The Best of
Mme. Jehane Benoit

Modern Canadian Library books are published by Pagurian Press Limited and are distributed in Canada by John Wiley and Sons Canada Limited, 22 Worcester Road, Rexdale, Ontario; and in the U.S.A. by Charles Scribner's Sons, 597 5th Avenue, New York, N.Y. 10017.

The Best of
Mme. Jehane Benoit

A collection of some of the most famous

recipes and ideas from Canada's best known cook and

most competent authority on Canadian foods.

MODERN CANADIAN LIBRARY
TORONTO

Printed and Bound in Canada

ISBN 0-919364-13-6

CONTENTS

DAINTY BEEF ROLLS

These finger-size rolls should be served hot with a half-and-half mixture of Dijon mustard and chili sauce, and small fingers of crustless rye bread.

½ lb. ground round
1 medium onion, grated
2 eggs
2 tsp. curry powder
½ tsp. cumin seeds
4 tbsp. fine dry bread crumbs
½ cup chopped fresh parsley
1 tsp. salt
salad oil

Place all ingredients except the oil in a bowl. Mix and knead until very smooth (or beat at medium speed in an electric mixer for 5 minutes). It must be worked until mixture is a smooth paste.

Wet your hands, take a small piece of mixture and roll between your palms to the shape of a little finger. Set on wax paper until all paste is rolled, then refrigerate.

To serve, heat oil in a frying pan over high heat. When hot, reduce heat to medium (or place pan on another burner at medium heat if you have an electric stove). Add a few meat fingers at a time (don't crowd them), and fry until golden, about 3-4 minutes each. Serves 8-10.

TERRINE DE CAMPAGNE

A terrine is a meat loaf with personality. A slice of this pâté with crusty French bread and a glass of light red wine is indeed an elegant hors d'oeuvre.

1 lb. lamb or pork liver
1 cup chopped onions
2 garlic cloves, crushed
¼ cup brandy
⅔ cup port wine
¼ lb. each ground veal and pork
1½ tsp. salt
½ tsp. pepper
1 bay leaf
1 tsp. each tarragon and thyme
2 eggs, beaten
strips of side bacon

With a sharp knife, coarsely chop the liver (don't grind it) and place in a non-metal bowl with the onion, garlic, brandy and port. Cover and refrigerate 24 hours to marinate.

Add remaining ingredients except bacon and mix thoroughly (an electric mixer can be used at medium speed for 5 minutes).

Line a terrine or an 8 x 5-inch loaf pan with strips of bacon. Pour in meat mixture, place in a pan of hot water and bake uncovered in a 350° oven for 1 hour. Turn heat to 300° and bake 30 minutes.

Remove from oven, cover with foil or wax paper and place a heavy object on top—the chefs use a brick, but a can of tomatoes or similar object can replace it. Refrigerate 12 hours, then unmold. A terrine will keep 2-3 weeks refrigerated, 2 months frozen. This will serve 12.

Variations: Replace the veal and pork with an equal amount of raw wild or domestic duck. Or when marinating the liver, add ½ lb. of coarsely chopped venison, sliced raw pheasant or partridge breasts. Make terrine as indicated, layering thin slices of pheasant or partridge between liver mixture. The baking time remains the same.

MUSHROOM ROLLS

These are served hot, 2 rolls per person, with crisp cooled sticks of celery. Prepare them ahead of time and keep refrigerated.

12 thin slices white bread
soft butter
½ lb. finely chopped fresh mushrooms
4 tbsp. butter
½ tsp. curry powder
1 tbsp. lemon juice
½ tsp. salt
¼ tsp. pepper

Remove crusts from bread and go over slices with a rolling pin to make them thinner. Spread with soft butter and set aside.

Melt 2 tbsp. of remaining butter with curry and lemon juice. Add mushrooms and sauté over high heat 3 minutes, stirring constantly. Sprinkle with the salt and pepper.

Spread about 1 tbsp. of mushrooms over each slice of bread. Roll like a jelly roll, fasten each roll with picks and place on a baking sheet. Melt last 2 tbsp. of butter, brush lightly over rolls and refrigerate. When ready to serve, bake in a 425° oven about 15 minutes, or until light brown. Serves 6.

BLUE CHEESE ROLL

As this will keep 3-4 weeks, have it handy for emergency appetizers or cocktail tidbits.

½ lb. Roquefort or Danish blue cheese
8-oz. pkg. cream cheese
3 tbsp. soft butter
3 tbsp. brandy
2 tbsp. minced chives or green onions
chopped roasted almonds
round unsalted crackers

Mash cheeses with butter, brandy and green onions or chives. When smooth and creamy, refrigerate for 1 hour. Form into a cylinder 1½ inches in diameter and roll in almonds. Wrap well and refrigerate. To serve, slice thinly and place on round crackers. Yield: 2½-3 dozen rounds.

CHEDDAR CHEESE WAFERS

These crisp cheese wafers are easy to prepare and, if stored in a metal box in a cool place, they will keep for months. Serve them hot or cold.

1 cup grated strong Cheddar cheese
1 cup crushed potato chips
¼ cup soft butter
½ cup all-purpose flour
1 tsp. prepared mustard

Measure the cheese and potato chips after grating or crushing. Place the cheese in a bowl, with the remaining ingredients and blend. Place on an unbuttered baking sheet in small spoonfuls, flattening slightly with the bottom of the spoon.

Bake at 375° for 5-8 minutes, or until golden brown, then cool on a cake rack. To serve hot, reheat at 300° for a few minutes.

LIPTAUER CHEESE

An Austrian delicacy given to me by a Viennese ballet dancer, part of my cooking repertoire for many years.

1-4-oz. pkg. cream cheese
2 tbsp. cream
1 tbsp. paprika
1 tsp. caraway seeds
1 tsp. capers
1 tbsp. chives

Blend all the ingredients thoroughly and serve with black bread. Serves 4 to 6.

SPECIAL SANDWICH SPREAD

Special because it's only 9 calories per tablespoon. Spread it (without butter) on melba toast, Rye-Krisp, whole wheat bread or, if you can afford 100 calories, use it in a roll.

4 medium carrots, scrubbed
½ green pepper, finely chopped (optional)
3 celery stalks, finely chopped
2 tbsp. chopped walnuts
2 tbsp. wheat germ
1 tbsp. prepared horseradish, well drained
3 tbsp. low-calorie mayonnaise-type dressing
1 tbsp. lemon juice
salt, to taste

Grate the carrots on the finest grater, add remaining ingredients and stir until well mixed. Refrigerate in a covered glass jar; it will keep 3 days. Yield: 2 cups.

PICKLED WILD MUSHROOMS

This was a contribution of the English settlers to Upper Canada's traditional cooking. Gathering wild mushrooms is a lost art, but this old recipe can be used for cultivated mushrooms with equal success and they make a most pleasant hors d'oeuvre or pickle.

Tie up in a piece of cheesecloth: several strips of parsley, pinch of thyme, a bay leaf, a whole clove, a dozen peppercorns. Put these in a saucepan with 2 cups water, 1 cup olive oil, ½ cup vinegar (I sometimes like to use lemon juice instead of vinegar). Let boil 5 minutes. Then add 1 lb. button mushrooms, the stems neatly clipped off, and let it all boil for 15 minutes. Remove from heat, take away spice bag, let mushrooms cool in juice. Pot, seal, and keep in a cool, dark place.

PICKLED MUSHROOMS

Each year I pickle 6-10 pints of little button mushrooms, which keep indefinitely under refrigeration. They can be served as an appetizer, as a condiment with fish or duck, or as a garnish to vegetables or rice salad.

3 lbs. small button mushrooms
cider vinegar
1 tsp. salt
salad oil
1 tbsp. mixed pickling spices *or*
1 tbsp. peeled fresh ginger, sliced

Rinse the whole unpeeled mushrooms in a colander under warm, then cold water. Place in a saucepan and cover with a mixture of half cider vinegar and half water (measure one cup of each, then add as needed). Add salt and boil for 15 minutes. Drain liquid into another pan and let the mushrooms cool.

Mix 1 cup cider vinegar with 1 cup salad oil and add spices. Fill sterilized jars ¼ full with the reserved liquid. Add mushrooms and pack down well. Fill jar to overflowing with the oil and vinegar mixture. Do this with the jar placed on a plate. Cover and refrigerate. Makes 2 pints.

DEVILLED ALMONDS

In winter, guests seem to love picking these right from the pan with their fingers. In the summer, you can serve them on plates, or let them cool.

4 tbsp. butter
1-1½ cups blanched almonds
1 tbsp. each chutney sauce, brown sugar and
Worcestershire sauce
½ tsp. each curry powder and turmeric
¼ tsp. salt
pinch of cayenne

Melt the butter in a 300° frypan and brown nuts, one layer deep, stirring and tossing often. Then blend remaining ingredients, add and stir with nuts until sugar is melted. Serves 6-8.

SOUPS

ABERDEEN BOUILLON

Bouillon has almost no calories and starting the dinner with a good cup of it not only cuts your appetite, but it makes the whole meal seem more important.

> **1 round shoulder beef bone* or 1 oxtail**
> **2 carrots, scrubbed and sliced**
> **1 celery stalk with leaves**
> **1 onion, diced**
> **1 bay leaf**
> **¼ tsp. thyme**
> **1 cup canned tomatoes with liquid**
> **8 cups cold water**
> **1 tsp. salt**
> **6 peppercorns**

Bring all the ingredients to a boil in a large saucepan; remove scum, if any. Cover and simmer 3 hours on low heat.

Strain, reserving meat and bone, then let cool. (You may use meat from the bone to make a salad). Pour liquid into quart jars, cover and refrigerate. When cold, the fat will rise to the top and can be removed in one piece; what's left is a delicious, clear, fat-free bouillon. Serve hot or cold as is, or garnish with minced celery, cucumber, parsley or green onions. Yield: 8 cups.

* Ask your butcher for a bone with some lean meat on it.

CONSOMME MAHARAJAH

Homemade chicken or beef consommé are the best. Diluted canned consommé can be used.

Place boiling hot consommé in a tureen on a tray, surround with the cups, a decanter of sherry, a bowl of grated cheese, herb biscuits, curried rice and petals of chrysanthemum. Each guest garnishes his own consommé to taste.

JAPANESE CONSOMME

Bring together to a boil an equal quantity of clam juice and undiluted consommé.

To serve, pour into small porcelain cups. Top with a pale pink rose petal.

CURRIED CONSOMME

A light, tasty soup to serve before chicken, duck or veal.

2 tbsp. butter
1 large onion, chopped
2 slices bacon, diced
1 tbsp. curry powder
1 tbsp. flour
6 cups bouillon (stock, canned or cubes)
1/3 cup uncooked long grain rice
1/3 cup parsley, minced
1/3 cup grated cheese

Fry onion and bacon together in butter. Add curry powder and stir until well blended. Add flour and blend. Add bouillon and rice. Stir well. Bring to the boil.

Cover and simmer over low heat 30 to 40 minutes. Serve in warm bowls. Sprinkle with parsley and grated cheese before serving. Serves 6.

LEEK BASE FOR VICHYSSOISE

Do this in the autumn when fresh leeks are plentiful and low in cost. Then a gourmet soup can be prepared in 20 minutes, all year round.

12 medium-sized leeks
4 large, mild onions
1½ cups butter

Remove top coarse leaves from leeks. Make a long split from the white part to the end of the green part. Wash carefully under running cold water, shaking off surplus water. Cut into thin slices, starting at the white base. Peel and slice the onions as thinly as possible. Melt the butter in a saucepan, add the leeks and onions, stir well for a few seconds. Cover and cook over very low heat for 25 minutes, stirring a few times. The mixture must soften completely but not brown. It will reduce quite a bit in proportion. Divide by cupfuls into containers and freeze. Yield: 3 pints.

To make the soup: Bring 3-4 cups chicken consommé to the boil, add 1 cup of the frozen leek mixture. Simmer 20 minutes. Beat in 1 cup instant mashed potatoes, previously stirred with ½ cup cold milk. Simmer together for a few minutes. Add 1 cup cream. When the soup is creamy, taste for seasoning and serve as is. The soup can be strained when ready, and refrigerated until cold.

CUCUMBER VICHYSSOISE

This quick soup can be made in a blender. Hot or cold, it is delicious.

1 can (10½ oz.) frozen cream of potato soup
½ cup milk
1 medium-size cucumber
½ cup heavy cream, or 1 cup commercial sour cream
minced fresh dill, or paprika, or watercress (if serving cold),
or minced chives (if serving hot)

Partially thaw the can of frozen cream of potato soup. Put the chunks in the container of a blender. Cover and mix at high speed.

Add milk and the cucumber which has been peeled, seeded, and cut into 2-inch pieces. Cover and blend for a few seconds.

Pour the mixture into a bowl and add heavy cream or sour cream. Taste for seasoning and stir well. Refrigerate until ready to serve.

When serving cold simply garnish with dill, paprika, or watercress. To serve hot, heat, and garnish with chives. Serves 4.

COLD CREAM OF CUCUMBER SOUP

This is a famous Polish summer soup. I often serve it with a bowl of boiled shrimps, cooled and stirred with a little French dressing—a complete light meal.

3 large cucumbers, peeled and thinly sliced
3 tbsp. butter
1 cup green beet tops, chopped
2 green onions, diced
3 tbsp. flour
salt, pepper to taste
4 cups chicken broth or consommé
½ cup rich cream
1-2 tbsp. chives, chopped
1 tbsp. fresh dill

In a saucepan, melt the butter, add the cucumbers, the beet tops and green onions. Simmer over low heat for 10 minutes, stirring a few times.

Sift the flour over the cucumbers, salt and pepper to taste, and stir together until well blended. Add the chicken broth or consommé. Stir until slightly thickened, then simmer over low heat for 15 minutes. Pass through a food mill or sieve, or blend in an electric blender. Taste for seasoning.

Refrigerate, covered, until cold. Add the cream, chives and dill. Serve well chilled. Serves 6.

FISH

CORNELL OVEN-FRIED FILLETS

This very interesting method was developed at Cornell University. It gives the crisp crust and browned flavor of pan-fried fish, yet uses less fat, requires less attention and causes almost no frying odors.

Partially thaw 1 lb. of fish fillets. Stir 1 tsp. of salt into ½ cup of milk. Mix 1 cup of fine, dry bread crumbs and 1 tsp. of paprika. Dip each portion of fish into the milk, then roll in the bread crumbs.

Oil, grease or butter (bacon fat is very nice) a shallow baking pan and arrange the crumbed fillets in it side by side. Drizzle 2 tbsp. of melted butter over them and bake uncovered in a preheated 500° oven 8-10 minutes, or until fish flakes when tested with a fork. Serve as is or with Tartar Sauce. Serves 3.

BROILED FROZEN FILLETS

To retain the flavor in broiled frozen fillets, start cooking them the moment their outside surface loses its icy rigidity, a point at which they're still a little difficult to separate. A quick searing under the broiler retains their flavor and moisture.

Preheat the broiler and grease the broiler pan only where it will be covered with the fish. Do not use a wire rack. Rub fillets with fresh lemon juice, then brush generously with melted butter, bacon fat or salad oil.

Arrange them in broiler pan and place 2 inches from source of heat. Without turning them, broil 8-12 minutes or a few minutes more if the fillets were hard frozen. Serve immediately.

ITALIAN BAKED FILLETS

Serve them with spinach and a tomato salad for a very interesting trio.

2 lbs. frozen fish fillets
1 cup commercial sour cream
½ cup chopped green onions
½ tsp. salt
¼ tsp. pepper
⅓ cup grated Parmesan cheese

Thaw fillets just enough to separate and place in well-greased shallow baking casserole. Combine remaining ingredients and spread evenly over each portion. Bake in a 350° oven 20-25 minutes, then sprinkle with paprika. Serves 6.

FISH HASH

When I have leftover fish and potatoes, I prepare this and refrigerate or freeze it to have on hand for a quick breakfast or lunch.

cold cooked fish fillets (at least 1 cup)
equal quantity cold boiled potatoes
1 large onion, grated
¼ tsp. sage
1 egg, beaten
3 tbsp. margarine

Flake the fish and cut the potatoes into small pieces. Mix with onion, add sage and beaten egg.

Melt margarine in a large frying pan. When hot, press the hash in and cook over medium heat until crusty brown underneath. Invert onto a hot platter and sprinkle to taste with minced parsley or green onions, or catsup. If the hash has been frozen, thaw it over low heat then raise heat to medium and continue.

BRAISED HADDOCK WITH SAVORY BALLS

This was one of my mother's favorites. A Scottish nanny we had for one of my brothers taught her how to make it, and it is a very interesting way to serve fish.

Braised Haddock:

7 slices bacon
1½ to 2 lbs. fillets of haddock
rind of 1 lemon, grated
½ tsp. salt
¼ tsp. freshly ground pepper

Line a baking dish with 4 slices of bacon. Top with the fillets of haddock. Spread 3 slices of bacon on top of the fish.

Mix the grated lemon rind with the salt and pepper. Sprinkle on top of fish and bacon.

Place the savory balls around the fish.

Cover the dish with its cover or a sheet of foil. Bake in a preheated 425° oven for 25 minutes. Uncover and bake for 5 minutes longer. Serves 6.

Savory Balls:

⅔ cup well-packed fresh bread crumbs
1 tbsp. dried parsley
¼ tsp. dried sage, or savory
1 small onion, minced
2 slices bacon, diced
½ tsp. salt
¼ tsp. pepper
2 eggs

Place in a bowl the bread crumbs, dried parsley, dried sage or savory, minced onion, diced bacon, salt, pepper and eggs.

Mash and blend with your hands until well mixed. Shape into small balls.

BROIL-POACHED HADDOCK

Fish is first on the list of any figure-conscious diet, so why not serve it once a week.

The following method is perfect because the oils cook out of the fish and yet the fish retains a rich trove of iodine and other minerals.

To keep to the diet idea, start the meal with a large bowl of iced, crisped celery, radishes, carrot sticks, green onions and a few olives.

> 4 1-inch thick haddock fillets or steaks
> 1 cup hot water
> 2 tbsp. fresh lemon juice
> 1 tsp. salt
> ½ tsp. pepper
> lemon sections
> chopped fresh parsley
> 3 tbsp. melted butter
> ¼ tsp. curry powder
> 1 minced green onion

Place the individual portions of fish in a shallow baking dish. **Mix** the water with the lemon juice, salt and pepper. Pour over the fish. Then place the fish under the broiler, about 4 inches from the heat. When the water comes to the boil, cook just 7 to 8 minutes. The top should be browned, the fish opaque and easily flaked off when touched with a fork. The water will be coated with oil. Lift the fish carefully with a wide-slotted spatula to a hot platter.

Melt the butter with the curry powder and green onion. Pour over fish and serve. Garnish with sections of lemon and sprinkle with the parsley. Serves 4.

SHRIMPS SUPERBA

Do not attempt to make these with frozen or canned shrimps. Large uncooked shrimps are a must. Cooked on the hibachi or in electric frying pan in front of your guests, followed by a tray of assorted cheeses, crisp crackers, homemade breads and a bottle of white wine, it makes a delectable do-it-yourself lunch.

1½ lbs. fresh shrimps
juice and grated rind from 2 limes
2 tsp. coarse salt
3 - 6 tbsp. salad oil
3 limes, quartered

Split the shrimps in half lengthwise through the shell and tail. Rinse out dark vein. Dry shrimps on paper towels, place on platter, cut side up, and sprinkle with the lime juice and grated rind and the salt. Cover with wax paper and refrigerate 3 to 6 hours.

To serve, heat the salad oil in large frying pan. Add half the shrimps at a time, skin side down, sauté until shells are pink, about 2 minutes per side, turning only once. Heap on warm platter, surround with the quartered limes, for everyone to use according to taste. Serves 4.

BARBECUED SHRIMP

A 7-pound box of frozen uncooked shrimps (purchased from a wholesale fish dealer) makes an exciting barbecue for 10, at less cost than steak. Try it some day.

2 - 3 lbs. uncooked shrimps
⅓ cup olive oil
⅓ cup plus 1 tsp. lemon juice
1½ tsp. curry powder
1 tsp. crushed garlic, or
½ tsp. garlic powder
1 tsp. salt
1 cup chutney
2 tbsp. brandy
hot bread

Rinse shrimps in cold water. If they are frozen, let them soak for 30 minutes and they will be easy to separate. Then shell and devein.

Stir together olive oil, ⅓ cup lemon juice, curry powder, garlic or garlic powder, and salt.

Add the shelled shrimps to the mixture and stir until well blended. Cover and refrigerate for 3 to 6 hours, stirring once or twice if possible. Then lift shrimps from marinade and strain and reserve the liquid.

Adjust the grill 3 inches from prepared hot coals. Place shrimps on the grill and cook for 5 minutes without turning, but basting several times with the marinade.

Mix chutney with the remaining 1 teaspoon lemon juice and brandy. Use as a dip. Serve grilled shrimps with the dip and plenty of hot bread. Serves 4-6.

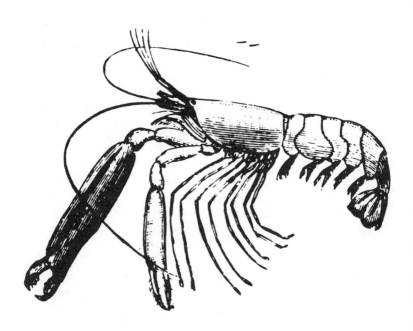

MEAT

ENGLISH BOILED KIDNEY PUDDING

This may seem involved to prepare but, once done, you'll realize how easy it is. A perfect cold-weather dish, it's a tradition of classic English cuisine.

1½ lbs. bottom round steak
1 beef kidney
1 tbsp. flour
1 onion, finely chopped
1¾ cups flour
½ tsp. salt
¼ cup fresh white bread crumbs
1 cup minced beef suet

Cut the beef and kidneys into ½-inch cubes. Roll them in the 1 tbsp. of flour mixed with salt and pepper to taste, mix in onion and set aside.

For the suet crust pastry, sift flour with salt into bowl. Add bread crumbs and stir in suet. Mix to a firm dough with about ½ cup of cold water. Grease a 1½-pint English pudding dish (that's a round, white bowl with a wide rim).

On a floured board, roll ⅔ of the pastry into a circle about 1 inch thick. Dust centre with flour, then fold circle in half. Make a 1-inch pleat in the middle of curved side, turn over and do same on other side so the dough will fit the round dish. Press bottom fold, rolling pin from bottom of pastry to top, not side to side.

Lift one edge of the pastry and put your fist inside the pocket — when you raise your hand you'll have the familiar "bonnet" you've seen cooks achieve. Lay pudding bowl on its side and carefully place pastry in it. Straighten bowl and, starting at the pleats, work edge of pastry so that it stands ½-1 inch above the top of the dish.

Pour in meat mixture and add cold water until dish is ¾ full. Dampen edge of pastry, roll a lid from remaining piece, place on pudding and pinch edges together well.

Dip a piece of clean cotton into hot water and wring out. Flour the inside, make a 1-inch pleat in the middle to allow for rising, and place over pudding. Tie around rim with a string, then loosely knot four corners of cloth back over top.

Submerge pudding in a large pan of rapidly boiling water, cover pan and boil steadily 3-4 hours. If necessary, add more hot water; the pudding should be covered by an inch or two of water at all times.

To serve, take off cloth and tie a folded napkin around dish. Place on table with a jug of boiling water, and when the first portion of pudding is cut, pour in a little water to increase and dilute the very rich, tasty gravy. Serves 6.

SCOTTISH BEEF AND KIDNEY PIE

This is quite different from the English type, and the beef kidney is often replaced by 3 or 4 lamb kidneys, or 2 veal kidneys. If you have a "little porcelain black bird" to use as a funnel, you'll be thoroughly traditional.

pie crust of your choice
1½ lbs. bottom round steak
1 small beef kidney
flour
1 tbsp. butter
1 large onion, chopped
1¼ cups boiling water
1 tsp. salt
¼ tsp. pepper
1 tbsp. Worcestershire sauce
1 tbsp. strong prepared mustard
2 tbsp. flour

Remove and reserve all fat from the steak and cut meat into ¾-inch cubes. Cut kidney into ¼-inch cubes and roll both meats in flour.

Melt fat from meat in a large frying pan, add butter and fry onion until golden brown. Gradually add beef and kidney, stirring over high heat until all rawness disappears, then remove to a heavy metal saucepan.

Add remaining ingredients to fat in pan, bring to a boil while stirring and pour over meat. Cover and simmer 1 hour, or until meat is tender. Let cool and, if you wish to de-fat the sauce, refrigerate overnight. The next day, remove fat on top and proceed.

Place a small funnel or a pie bird in the centre of a deep, 10-inch round baking dish, preferably one with a ½-inch rim. Pour in meat and about half the gravy. Roll enough pastry to cover the top, making a hole in the middle to pass over the funnel or bird, and brush with milk. Bake in a 425° oven 30-35 minutes, or until golden brown. Reheat leftover gravy and serve in sauceboat. Serves 6.

CHINESE PEPPER STEAK

This colorful, tasty dish counts 281 calories per portion, but you can also indulge in 100-calories' worth of plain boiled rice and still have very little calorie intake for such a good meal.

1 lb. lean top sirloin
1 cup celery, thinly sliced on bias
1 large onion, thinly sliced
1 garlic clove, crushed
2-3 green peppers, in thin slivers
1 tbsp. salad oil
1 cup bouillon or canned undiluted consommé
1 tbsp. cornstarch blended with
¼ cup water and
2 tbsp. soya sauce

Slice the meat very thinly, then cut in thin strips. Make sure all the vegetables are prepared before you start to cook; this dish will be ready to serve in 8-10 minutes.

Heat salad oil in large frying pan. Add beef and sear quickly over high heat, stirring most of the time. All this should take only 1 minute; remove beef from pan while it's still rare.

Add vegetables and consommé to pan and stir over high heat 3-4 minutes until tender-crisp. Add blended cornstarch, water and soya sauce, stirring until creamy. When very hot, add beef and reheat for a minute. Serves 4.

FRENCH BRAISED BEEF

This thick round steak with its intriguing flavor becomes a company dish when served with pommes vertes: equal quantities of mashed potatoes and cooked spinach beaten together until pale green, then seasoned to taste. Perfect fare for the electric frypan.

2½-3 lb. piece bottom round of beef
2 tbsp. salad oil
6 thin slices side bacon or fat salt pork, diced
paprika, to taste
4 carrots, in 1-inch pieces
4 onions, thinly sliced
2 whole cloves, finely chopped
½ tsp. thyme
¼ tsp. sage
peel of 1 orange, in slivers

Remove and dice all visible fat from the beef while heating frypan to 350°. Heat fat, oil, and bacon or salt pork in pan and, when suet is brown, sprinkle one side of meat with paprika and place that side down in fat. Brown until golden, then sprinkle with paprika, turn and brown other side, 20-25 minutes in all.

Add carrots, onions broken into rings, and seasonings, being careful there's no white on the orange skin. Salt and pepper to taste. Swish together a bit, and cook covered at 325° for 1½ hours, or until meat is tender.

Remove meat to a hot serving platter. To thicken sauce, either mash vegetables in the pan juices, or pass them through a sieve and return to pan with ½ cup of sour cream. Warm up, but don't let mixture boil, then pour over meat. Serves 8.

BOILED BEEF VINAIGRETTE

Periodically, I have boiled beef, which should be called simmered beef, as it must never boil if you like the meat tender and compact instead of dry and stringy. The contrast of hot meat and cold sauce gives this dish its character.

3-4 lbs. beef brisket, *or*
4 lbs. short ribs, in 1 piece
3 celery ribs, cut into 2-inch lengths
6 carrots, cut into halves
6 whole onions
6 small whole parsnips
½ tsp. ground thyme
1 bay leaf
2 tsp. salt
¼ tsp. pepper
8-10 small new potatoes
¼ cup cider or tarragon vinegar
½ cup minced parsley
3 tbsp. minced dill
2 tbsp. minced chives
2 tsp. salt
½ tsp. pepper
¼ tsp. dry mustard
½ tsp. sugar
½ cup olive oil

Place the meat in a large saucepan. Add the celery, carrots, onions, parsnips, thyme, bay leaf and seasoning. Add boiling water to cover the whole. Cover tightly and simmer gently for 4 to 5 hours, or until meat is tender.

About 30 minutes before the meat is ready, take out 2 to 3 cups of the bouillon and place in a saucepan. Scrub the potatoes and cook them in their jackets in the bouillon.

Prepare the vinaigrette a few hours ahead, if you prefer, or at the last minute — place the remaining ingredients in a bowl and stir for a minute or two.

Set the meat on a hot platter, place the carrots, onions, parsnips and potatoes around the meat, and pour a few spoonfuls of the vinaigrette over the meat and serve the rest cold in an attractive bowl. Serves about 8.

BRAISED RED WINE CHUCK STEAK

A low cost cut becomes a dish of haute cuisine when prepared as follows. Nice served with baked potatoes and onions that will cook in the same period of time as the meat in the oven.

3-3½ lbs. thick beef chuck steak
1 large onion, thinly sliced
1 small carrot, thinly sliced
1 cup red wine (any type)
½ tsp. each basil and thyme
2 tbsp. brown sugar
3 tbsp. beef or bacon fat
1 or 2 cloves garlic, chopped fine
salt and pepper to taste
2 tbsp. flour
1 tbsp. chili sauce
juice of 1 orange
chopped parsley or chives

Put the steak in a bowl, top with the onion, carrot, red wine, basil and thyme. Cover and marinate overnight. When ready to cook remove the meat from mixture, wipe it off, reserving the marinade.

Melt the brown sugar and fat together in heavy metal frying pan. Sear the meat in it, on all sides over medium heat. Then place in a casserole or Dutch oven. Add the marinade mixture to the frying pan. Heat while scraping the bottom of the pan. When it boils, pour it over the meat. Add the garlic, salt and pepper to taste. Cover and bake half an hour in a 325° oven. Turn the heat down to 300° and bake 1 hour. Turn the meat over and bake 1½ hours longer or until meat is tender. Remove the meat from the pan. Stir together the flour, chili sauce and orange juice. Add to sauce, whisk thoroughly, then put the sauce through a sieve (if you prefer, leave sauce with vegetables in it). Bring to boil while stirring. Pour a few spoonfuls over the meat. Sprinkle top with parsley. Serve the rest of the sauce separately. Serves 8.

SUPER HAMBURGER

To obtain perfect results with these, please follow the exact directions for the meat. They are so good when well made that they can be used for a company dinner. In the summer, I enjoy them broiled on the barbecue with roasted fresh corn.

2 lbs. round steak
3-inch square of beef suet
1 tsp. seasoned salt
1 tsp. plain salt
½ tsp. freshly ground pepper
3 tbsp. minced parsley
½ tsp. minced fresh or dried thyme
2 cups red wine

Have the butcher pass the steak and suet 3 times through the chopper.

As soon as you get home, place in a bowl and add the seasoned salt, plain salt, pepper, parsley and thyme. Mix lightly with a fork. Pour the red wine over, but do not mix. Cover and refrigerate all day.

When ready to cook, mix the wine with the meat. Shape into 6 large flat patties. Brown in butter; do not overcook. Serve with hot French bread and a green salad. Serves 6.

SMOKED BEEF TONGUE

This is an excellent dish for a buffet supper because it can be kept warm in a chafing dish. The tongue can be cooked days ahead of time, then sliced and simmered in the wine-cranberry sauce. Serve it with rice, noodles or pan-fried potatoes.

1 smoked beef tongue (about 2 lbs.)
1-inch piece fresh ginger root (optional)
3 slices unpeeled lemon
2 bay leaves
½ tsp. peppercorns
½ cup dark brown sugar

1 cup fresh cooked cranberries or
canned sauce plus juice of ½ a lemon
12 whole cloves
¼ cup dry red wine or sherry
½ unpeeled lemon, thinly sliced

Wash tongue, cover with cold water and let stand 3-5 hours. Drain, place in saucepan with enough cold water to cover, the ginger (don't use powdered), 3 lemon slices, bay leaves and pepper-corns. Bring to a boil, cover and simmer over low heat 3-4 hours, or until tender (it's cooked when the skin can be removed). Let cool, then cut off back part of tongue. If cooking ahead of time, wrap and refrigerate until ready to use.

Simmer brown sugar, cranberries, cloves and wine or sherry 5 minutes. Add lemon slices and paper-thin slices of cooked tongue. Keep warm over low heat. Serves 6-8.

FINNISH JELLIED TONGUE

A Finnish friend taught me how to cook this superb tongue dish that is prepared with jellied sour cream and garnished with feathery stems of fresh dill. It is a pleasant change from the usual type of meat served at buffet dinners.

1 fresh beef tongue
2 tbsp. sugar
1 tbsp. coarse salt
6-8 cups hot water
1 bay leaf
1 unpeeled lemon, thinly sliced
5-6 slices fresh ginger root or
1 tsp. ground ginger
1 quart cold water
3 tbsp. coarse salt
1 tbsp. sugar
1 envelope unflavored gelatin
juice of 1 lemon
1 cup sour cream
fresh dill or parsley

Mix the 2 tbsp. sugar and the 1 tbsp. salt together well and rub evenly over the tongue. Cover, and refrigerate overnight.

The next day, place the tongue in a large saucepan with the hot water and add the bay leaf, sliced lemon, ginger root or ground ginger. Bring to a fast rolling boil, skim off the foam, then cover and simmer over low heat for 2-3 hours until the tongue is tender. Skin the tongue while hot and let it cool in its broth.

In the meantime, bring to a boil 1 quart cold water with 3 tbsp. salt and 1 tbsp. sugar. Let cool, then add the cooled tongue. Refrigerate for 12 hours. Drain thoroughly and place on a flat platter.

Soak the unflavored gelatin in the lemon juice for 5 minutes and then dissolve over hot water. Slowly add to the sour cream, while stirring, and spread the cold tongue with this cream. Garnish with sprigs of fresh dill or parsley and refrigerate for 1 hour to set the gelatin. To serve, slice thinly. Serves 6-8.

OXTAIL CASSEROLE

Unusual and very tasty. Can be made two or three days before serving. Keep refrigerated. Also freezes well for 2 months. Reheat in a preheated 400° oven.

2 oxtails cut in 2-inch pieces
3 tbsp. butter
2 cans undiluted consommé
1 large onion, sliced thin
1 clove garlic, minced
1 green pepper, diced
1 small can tomatoes
3 small carrots, sliced thin
1 tsp. salt
6 peppercorns
1 tsp. brown sugar
¼ tsp. basil
⅛ tsp. marjoram
a pinch thyme
1 cup red wine
1 tsp. lemon juice

Brown the oxtails in butter over high heat. Place in an earthenware casserole and cover with the consommé. Brown the onion and garlic in the butter remaining in the pan. Spread over the oxtails. Add the rest of the ingredients. Cover the casserole and cook in a 325° oven 3 to 4 hours or until the oxtails are tender.

To serve, place 6 to 8 small boiled potatoes, rolled in finely minced parsley, around the meat. Serves 4-6.

COLD BEEF SALAD

The French, Italians and Mexicans make this salad with slight variations, but its country of origin is Greece. It is a good way to use up leftover beef.

1-2 lbs. thinly sliced cold beef
1 very thinly sliced mild onion
2 tbsp. capers
3 tbsp. minced parsley
½ tsp. marjoram
¼ cup salad oil
⅛ cup cider vinegar
1 tsp. prepared mustard
½ tsp. salt

Place the sliced meat in a deep platter. Break the onion into rings and drop on top of meat. Sprinkle onions with the capers, and the capers with parsley and marjoram.

Mix together the remaining ingredients, shake well and pour over the salad. Cover loosely and let stand for 3 hours, then refrigerate if you are not ready to serve. Garnish with lettuce or watercress. Serves 6.

EASTER LEG OF LAMB

Every Easter Sunday for many years we had dinner at the home of my maternal grand-mère. She had a very special way to braise a leg of lamb, which I have never found anywhere. Try it if you like a fat-free gravy and tender moist lamb.

5- to 6-lb. of lamb
1 cup water
1 tbsp. butter
1 onion, stuck with 3 cloves
1 large carrot, sliced
2 slices of unpeeled lemon
2 celery stalks, diced
8-10 parsley sprigs, chopped
1 tsp. minced basil, or oregano
1 tsp. salt
½ tsp. pepper
1 cup consommé (any type)
½ cup red wine
½ cup light or heavy cream
2 tbsp. browned flour

Place the leg of lamb in a roasting pan with the water. Cover and cook over high heat on top of the stove until the water has evaporated.

Uncover, add the butter, and still over high heat, brown the meat all over. Remove the lamb from the pan and discard all the accumulated fat from the pan.

Place in the bottom of the pan the onion, carrot, lemon slices, celery, parsley, and basil or oregano. Stir until well mixed. Place the lamb on top of these vegetables. Add salt and pepper to taste. Add the consommé. Cover and simmer over very low heat for 1½ hours.

Blend together the wine, cream and browned flour. Pour over lamb. Stir around until well mixed with all the ingredients. Cover and simmer for another 30 minutes.

Remove the meat to a hot platter. Strain the gravy and serve it separately. Serves 6-8.

MINT-PEPPERCORN ROAST SHOULDER OF LAMB

I like to make the required cup of broth with bones removed from the shoulder. When available, use Malabar black peppercorns. They are the most perfumed and flavorful.

1 whole shoulder of lamb
8-10 peppercorns
1 tsp. salt
¼ cup salad oil or melted butter
1 bunch green onions, coarsely chopped
8 stalks fresh mint, coarsely chopped or
1 tbsp. dried mint
1 cup broth, any type

Preheat the oven to 350°.

Place the peppercorns in a piece of cotton and crush them with a rolling pin or a potato masher. Place the meat in a dripping pan and rub it all over with the salt and ½ tsp. of the crushed peppercorns.

Roast the meat uncovered for 20 minutes, then pour the oil or melted butter on top. Continue roasting uncovered for 20 minutes, per pound. When 20 minutes remain, cover the meat with the green onion and mint, then add the broth to the pan.

When the meat is done, remove it from the oven and baste for 1-2 minutes with the pan drippings. Place the roast on a hot platter and serve the gravy as is, or thicken it to taste with 1 tbsp. of flour. Serves 8.

JACK'S BARBECUED LAMB SHANKS

My friend Jack preferred beer to rye! He called it the "new dimension flavor".

2 cloves garlic
4-6 lamb shanks
3 tbsp. melted lamb fat or bacon fat
3 tbsp. flour
½ tsp. salt
½ tsp. freshly ground pepper
½ tsp. savory
½ cup beer
2 bay leaves
¼ cup fresh lemon juice
grated peel of ½ a lemon

Put slivers of the garlic into the lamb shanks, make incisions with a pointed knife. Melt the pieces of lamb fat or heat the bacon fat in a Dutch oven. Blend the flour, salt, pepper and savory. Roll shanks into it and brown all over in the hot fat. Then add all the other ingredients. Cover and simmer for 2 hours or until meat is tender. The more it simmers, the more gravy forms. Serve as he did with boiled rice loaded with butter, parsley and sliced fried mushrooms. Serves 4-6.

NANNY'S "HONEST IRISH STEW"

Clara, who was our nanny when we were children, was actually French, but she had an Irish mother. As it turned out, she cared very little for cooking, no doubt because she had her hands full with her boisterous charges. But every now and then a spark of interest would flare up enthusiastically whenever she talked of or made one of her mother's "famous" Irish dishes. The mother had brought from Ireland, as part of her dowry, a very special little book. This contained recipes which had been meticulously written out by her grandmother, who had passed it on to her mother. Eventually, the book was given to Clara as the eldest daughter when, as Clara put it, her mother had "left this world to live in glory with the angels".

Among the things I learned from Clara and her little book was how to make "Honest Irish Stew". Whenever any of us had a cold, Clara always insisted that eating "Honest Irish Stew" was the only thing that would cure us. Here is the recipe.

3 lbs. neck of lamb
12 medium even-sized potatoes
4 large onions, sliced thick
salt and pepper
½ tsp. ground thyme
2 cups cold water

Only the neck will do, and so much the better, since it is a low-priced cut. It usually comes with lamb-in-the-basket. Ask your butcher to reserve 3 pounds of lamb neck in advance — it really is worth the trouble.

Remove excess fat from the meat, if necessary, and then cut into sections through the bones. Your butcher can also do this for you, but do not let him remove the bones as these are necessary for the final flavor.

Peel the potatoes and cut four of them into thin slices, as for scalloped potatoes. Leave the rest whole.

In the bottom of a heavy metal saucepan or casserole, place the sliced potatoes, then half of the sliced onions, and top this with the pieces of lamb. Season generously with salt and pepper. Sprinkle the rest of the onions with the thyme and place them on top of the lamb. Surround them with the remainder of the potatoes, left whole. Pour the cold water on top. Cover tightly. Poach in a 350° oven for 2½ hours, or simmer over very low heat for the same length of time. The sliced potatoes thicken the juice and the top ones, left whole, retain their shape and will be cooked just right. Makes 6 servings.

Clara used to serve her Irish stew with 3 small bowls, separately filled with capers, good homemade mustard, and chopped parsley. In the summer you can replace the parsley with chives.

Note: If it is not possible for you to obtain the neck of the lamb, despite any amount of effort on your part, you can replace it with an equal weight of lamb-in-the-basket.

VEAL CHOPS TOSCANINI

This dish was created for the great Maestro at a dinner that followed the unforgettable Wagner concert he directed in honor of Cosima Wagner, then a very old lady. As a student in Paris at the time, I had the joy of being at the concert and being invited to the superb midnight dinner that followed.

4 thick loin veal chops
4 thin slices of bacon
¾ cup grated Swiss cheese
pepper
3 tbsp. butter
salt to taste
4 ripe tomatoes, peeled
½ tsp. sugar
½ tsp. crumbled dried thyme
butter
juice of 1 lemon

In the side of each chop make an incision large enough to form a sort of small pocket. Dice the bacon; for each chop, mix one fourth of the diced bacon with 1 teaspoon of grated cheese. Pepper the inside of the pocket and fill with the bacon and cheese.

Melt the butter in a heavy enamelled cast-iron frying pan. When light brown, add the chops and brown for 5 minutes on each side, turning only once. Add salt and pepper to taste, cover, and let the chops cook over very low heat for 15 minutes.

In the meantime, place the peeled whole tomatoes in a shallow baking dish and sprinkle with the sugar and thyme. Place in a 450° oven for 5 minutes.

Top each tomato with a veal chop. Pour over the chops any juices accumulated in the pan. Sprinkle the whole with the remaining grated cheese and 8 to 10 small dice of butter. Put back in the oven until the cheese is melted and chops are crusty brown on top.

Remove from the oven and pour the juice of the lemon on top. Serves 4.

MUSHROOM VEAL LOAF

This can be served hot or cold. Make it a month ahead and freeze, or a week ahead and refrigerate.

1 lb. veal, minced
1 lb. uncooked ham, minced
4 tbsp. catsup
3 tbsp. chopped green pepper
1 medium-size onion, grated
2 eggs
1 tsp. salt
¼ cup fine, dry breadcrumbs
1 cup undiluted mushroom soup
1 cup fresh or canned mushrooms, fried

Thoroughly mix all ingredients except mushrooms and pour half of mixture into a 9 x 5-inch loaf pan. Cover with mushrooms and top with remaining mixture. Bake 1 hour in a 350° oven and let cool. Cover with foil and freeze, or refrigerate.

To serve, place in 350° oven and bake covered until heated through—about 1 hour if frozen, 40 minutes if it's been refrigerated, then unmold. Serves 6.

CHINESE BRAISED LOIN OF PORK

Use a cast iron or an electric frying pan to cook this. The meat glazes to a deep brown color and has an intriguing flavor without being too exotic.

3-4 lb. loin of pork
1 finely chopped garlic clove
1 tsp. salt
¼ tsp. pepper
2 tbsp. honey
¼ cup soya sauce
1 cup beef broth
2 tbsp. dry sherry

Bone the loin by detaching the meat from the bones and tying it into a neat roll, or leave the bone in if you prefer.

Rub the pork with a mixture of the garlic, salt and pepper. Brown it over medium heat on all sides, beginning with the fat side. Mix remaining ingredients, bring to a boil and pour over meat. Cover and cook over low (250°-300°) heat 1½ hours, or until tender, basting 3-4 times during cooking. Serve with plain or fried rice. Serves 6.

AMERICAN CHOP SUEY

Yes, a pound of boneless pork will serve 4-6 people. Take the meat from chops, or use tenderloin.

1 lb. lean boneless pork
2 tbsp. salad oil
¼ cup hot water
6-8 green onions, in 1-inch pieces
1½ cups slivered celery
5-oz. can water chestnuts, thinly sliced
1 cup chicken broth
1 tbsp. soya sauce
1 tbsp. cornstarch

38

Cut the meat into thin strips. Heat the oil in a large, heavy frying pan, add meat and stir over medium heat until rawness disappears. Add hot water, cover and simmer 20 minutes over lowered heat.

Add onions, celery, chestnuts, broth, and simmer covered 15 minutes. Add combined soya sauce and cornstarch, stirring until slightly thickened. Taste for seasoning and serve with rice. Serves 4.

COATED ROAST PORK

The coating, low heat and long cooking period seal the juices into the pork and result in a tender, tasty roast.

2-3 lbs. shoulder pork
4 tbsp. soya sauce
1 tbsp. sherry
1 tbsp. cornstarch
¼ tsp. pepper
¼ tsp. monosodium glutamate
2 garlic cloves, crushed

Preheat the oven to 275° and place roast on a rack in a dripping pan.

Blend together the remaining ingredients and spread this mixture over the entire surface of the meat. Roast 45-50 minutes per pound. The meat will then be crisp on the outside, but tender and juicy on the inside. Serve either hot or cold. Serves 4-6.

ROAST STUFFED PORK TENDERLOIN

Pork tenderloin is an ideal cut when a small roast is required. It is equally good hot or cold.

1¼ to 1½ lbs. pork tenderloin
½ recipe for Citrus Dressing (page 99)
½ tsp. salt
¼ tsp. pepper
½ tsp. curry powder

Beat the tenderloin with the flat side of a cleaver to flatten it, then slit into two without detaching the two pieces. Fill with dressing and tie securely.

Mix the salt, pepper, and curry powder. Rub all over the stuffed tenderloin. Place on a well-oiled roasting pan without a rack, insert a meat thermometer into the center. Do not cover the meat; do not wrap in foil; do not add water. Bake in a 325° oven until the thermometer registers 185°, or for 35 minutes to the pound.

Serve with browned potatoes and broccoli with butter and lemon juice. Serves about 4.

THAILAND PORK TENDERLOIN

This is a colorful and tasty dish One tenderloin can serve 6, simply by adding more vegetables to the recipe.

1 or 2 pork tenderloin
2 eggs, beaten
3 tbsp. cornstarch
1 carrot, in thin shreds
1 green pepper, in thin shreds
½ cup slivered celery
2 tbsp. sugar
2 tbsp. vinegar
1 bouillon cube
1 cup hot water
4 tbsp. salad oil

Cut the tenderloin in ½-inch cubes. Roll them in the beaten eggs and then the cornstarch. Set on wax paper to dry.

Place the vegetables, sugar, vinegar, bouillon cube and hot water in a bowl, stirring to dissolve the bouillon cube. Set aside for 30 minutes. Be sure to increase the quantity of vegetable ingredients if you are using only one tenderloin.

Heat the oil in a large frying pan. Add the pieces of tenderloin and brown quickly over high heat, stirring all the time. Add the vegetable mixture and stir 2-3 minutes over medium heat. Serve immediately with a bowl of boiled rice. Serves 6.

GREEK PIKTI

The pikti are the jellied pig's feet of Greece, very similar to the pork head cheese of Quebec, although more delicate in flavor. They are served as appetizers or a cold main course.

4 pig's feet, cut up
1 tbsp. salt
4 onions, sliced
2 carrots, whole
1 cup celery, chopped
1 bay leaf
3 whole cloves
1 tsp. peppercorns
½ tsp. oregano
½ cup pimiento, diced
3 tbsp. cider or wine vinegar
½ cup fresh parsley, minced

Place the pig's feet in a large saucepan and cover with boiling water and the salt. Cover and simmer 2 hours, then remove any scum that has accumulated on top.

Add the onions, carrots, celery, bay leaf, cloves, peppercorns and oregano. Bring back to a boil, cover and simmer for 1 hour, or until the meat is falling from the bones. Remove the meat and the carrots from the bouillon and set aside.

Strain the broth, put it back in the pan and boil until reduced by one third. Pick the meat from the bones and chop coarsely or finely, according to taste. Don't discard the skin, chop it with the rest of the meat. Dice the carrots and add with the pimiento to the meat. Pour it all into the reduced broth and simmer together 5 minutes.

Remove from heat, add the vinegar and parsley and pour into 3-4 molds. Cool, cover and refrigerate until firm. To serve, unmold and garnish with parsley and quarters of lemon. Serves 8-10.

BARBECUED SPARERIBS

A most versatile recipe. Cook the spareribs in one piece or cut into 2-inch pieces. Bake or broil in the oven or barbecue over charcoal. The flavor and crispness, although different with each method, remain perfect.

1 or 2 cloves garlic, crushed
½ cup soya sauce
⅓ cup sugar or honey
1 tbsp. grated orange peel
1 tsp. salt
¼ tsp. pepper
2½-3 lbs. spareribs

Mix garlic, soya sauce, sugar or honey, salt, pepper and orange peel.

Trim excess fat from spareribs, use pieces whole or cut in 2-inch lengths. Place meat in a shallow pan, spread with the garlic mixture. Let stand covered in refrigerator, 1 to 24 hours, turning meat 2 or 3 times.

To broil the meat: place whole piece, curved side down, on rack in baking pan. If the meat is cut, place the squares next to each other. Preheat broiler at 325° for 15 minutes, place the pan 6 to 8 inches from the medium flame for about 20 minutes. When meat is crusty and brown on one side, turn it and continue cooking until the other side is browned and the meat is tender.

To bake: place in shallow dripping pan, without rack, in 400° oven. Broiled or baked, cooking time is 40 to 60 minutes. Serves 4.

STUFFED SPARERIBS

I have never been able to decide if I prefer these hot or cold. Either way they are superb. If you roast them early in the morning, place them on a platter, cover with foil and let stand until dinner time. They will be tepid, moist and so good.

3-4 lbs. pork spareribs
1 tsp. salt
¼ tsp. pepper
2½ cups bread, diced
3 tbsp. soft butter
2 eggs

salt and pepper, to taste
1 tsp. sage or savory
¼ cup parsley, chopped
2 cups cider or water

Use a whole rack of spareribs or 2 of equal size. Rub them with salt and pepper. In a bowl, combine the bread, butter, eggs, salt, pepper, sage or savory and parsley. Mix well and place over the spareribs. If using 1 rack of spareribs, fold them over and sew the ends together, or secure them with skewers. When 2 pieces are used, place stuffing on one and cover with the other. Tie securely together with string.

Place the ribs in a roasting pan with the cider or water. Bake at 450° for 1 hour, turning every 20 minutes. If meat browns too much, turn heat down to 350°. Serves 6.

RUM HAM

The combination of rum, oranges and brown sugar makes a delicious glaze on the ham. Even though this takes time to cook, it requires only a little attention from you, which makes it a good dish for a party.

1 ham, any size
1-2 tsp. whole cloves
1 cup brown sugar
3 oranges, unpeeled
1½ cups rum

Wrap a ham of your choice in heavy-duty foil. Bake in a 300° oven for 35 minutes to the pound. (Any size ham can be baked this way.)

About 1 hour before ham is done, remove from the foil. Remove the rind with a sharp knife and score the fat. Stud with cloves. Pack brown sugar on top.

Slice unpeeled oranges. Place them in the bottom of the baking pan. Set the ham on the bed of oranges. Slowly pour rum on top.

Return the pan to the oven for 1 hour. Baste the ham a few times with the liquid in the pan. This makes a different and tasty dish for a buffet supper.

A 6-lb. boneless fully cooked ham will make 8 to 10 servings.

HAM LOAF

This one's quicker than cooking a whole ham. Serve it thinly sliced, with fresh Onion Cucumber Relish and rye bread, plus assorted fruits and cheese for dessert.

1½ lbs. ground cooked or uncooked ham
¾ lb. ground fresh pork
3 eggs, slightly beaten
½ cup undiluted cream of celery soup
½ tsp. marjoram or curry powder
½ tsp. dry mustard
1 cup dry bread crumbs

Mix all ingredients, following given order. (No salt is needed as the ham and soup have enough.) Put into a 9 x 5-inch loaf pan and bake uncovered in a 350° oven for 1¼ hours. Let cool, cover and refrigerate (it will keep 4 days), or freeze (3 months).

To reheat, thaw completely if frozen, place uncovered in a 350° oven for 30 minutes. Serves 6.

CRISP STEAM-BAKED CHICKEN

Serve it with a green salad, or with celery and carrot sticks. It's 175 calories per quarter-chicken—without the gravy!

3-lb. broiler
½ tsp. salt
pinch of garlic powder
½ tsp. tarragon or basil
¼ tsp. pepper
paprika

Quarter chicken and place in a shallow baking dish, skin-side up. Mix all ingredients except paprika and sprinkle over. Sprinkle generously with paprika. Cover, using foil if you have no lid, and bake in a 350° oven 1½ hours, or until golden. Serves 4.

CHICKEN CATALAN

Another marriage of fresh lemon and chicken, which produces a light, fresh, delightful chicken casserole. The Catalans serve it with broiled tomatoes, heavily sprinkled with minced chives, and hot French bread.

3- to 4-lb. chicken
4 tbsp. butter
salt and pepper
2-3 garlic cloves
3 lemons, unpeeled
¼ tsp. crumbled dried thyme
1 bay leaf
1 cup chicken consommé
1 tbsp. cornstarch
¼ cup cold heavy cream

Cut chicken into individual pieces. Heat butter in a casserole and brown the chicken in it. Add salt and pepper to taste.

Crush garlic cloves and add them to the chicken; stir until the garlic is brown here and there.

Cut unpeeled lemons into very thin slices. Add to the chicken with thyme and bay leaf. Add consommé. Bring to a boil, cover, and cook over medium heat until chicken is tender, 40 to 60 minutes.

Place the chicken on a deep hot serving platter. Arrange the lemon slices over the chicken, but discard the bay leaf. Stir cornstarch with cold heavy cream. Add to the liquid in the casserole and stir over medium heat until the sauce is creamy and transparent. Strain the sauce over the chicken. Serves 4-6.

MY FAVORITE BROILED CHICKEN

You will find that this dish is very nice when it is served cold, but it is even better when it has not been refrigerated first.

1 broiler (2½ to 3 lbs.)
salt and pepper
3 tbsp. salad oil
1 tsp. paprika
½ tsp. crumbled dried tarragon, basil, or savory, _or_
¼ tsp. ground thyme or sage

Separate the chicken into halves with poultry shears or a pair of good kitchen scissors. It's easy. Start by cutting down the back first, then turn and cut through the breast bone. Remove the backbone and the neck and use these for chicken stock. Twist the wing joints in their sockets so the pieces will lie flat.

Place the bird skin side down directly on the broiler pan, not on a rack. Sprinkle the top with salt and pepper, pour the salad oil on top, and sprinkle with paprika. If you happen to like herbs, sprinkle on the herb of your choice.

Place the broiler pan in the lowest part of the preheated broiler, as far as possible from the source of heat. Broil on one side for 30 minutes, then turn, and baste the top with the juices in the pan. Broil on the other side for another 30 minutes, or until skin is crisp and golden brown. After 15 minutes, lower the heat if the skin is browning too rapidly.

The chicken is now ready to serve. It is so good that I never serve any type of sauce with it. I suggest only a large bowl of crisp cool green salad and a bottle of chutney. Serves 4.

ST. BONIFACE PICNIC BROILERS

Although this was served outside at what was called "A French pioneer barn raising," it can easily be duplicated with oven broilers.

6 broilers
½ cup salad oil
juice of 2 lemons
½ tsp. salt
½ tsp. marjoram
¼ tsp. pepper
12-14 potatoes

The day before the picnic have the broilers dressed and cut in halves. Brush each half broiler with a mixture of oil, lemon juice, salt, marjoram, and pepper. Lay halves in wax paper lined roaster or large dish — one on top of the other, and cover with wax paper. Refrigerate overnight. Before packaging for picnic, brush again with oil mixture.

When the fire is a gray mass of coals, place chicken, bone side first, on oiled broiler. Brown 15 minutes, turn and cook until skin is brown and crisp. Then place pieces in roaster, cover and allow to remain in a just-warm spot on the grill, 15 to 20 minutes. Just before serving, brush the birds with the remaining oil mixture.

Wrap the potatoes in foil and bake in the gray coals for 35 to 40 minutes. Serves 12.

MONIQUE'S ROAST CHICKEN MEAL

My daughter, Monique, has many good tricks for preparing quick tasty dinners. This is one of her family's favorites.

4-6 chicken legs
1 tsp. salt
½ tsp. tarragon or savory
1 tsp. turmeric
¼ tsp. pepper
1 tbsp. flour
½ cup fat (any type)
8-12 baking powder biscuits
3 tsp. flour
⅔-1 cup milk

Cut the chicken legs in two. On a plate, or in a paper bag, mix together the salt, tarragon or savory, turmeric, pepper and flour. Roll the chicken in it. Melt the fat (Monique's favorite is half butter, half bacon fat) in a large baking dish or dripping pan. Place the chicken legs in it and bake 20 minutes in a 375° oven. Turn and bake another 20 minutes, then move the pieces to one side of the dish.

Prepare the biscuits from a ready-mix or your own favorite recipe while the chicken is cooking. Place next to the chicken and bake 15 minutes in a 400° oven. Remove both chicken and biscuits to a hot platter. Add 3 tsp. of flour to remaining fat in pan. Stir well, add the milk and cook over direct heat until creamy and smooth. Serve separately or pour over chicken. Serves 4.

CHICKEN WINGS "A LA HOUSTON"

My friend Houston is a publisher and a great cook. This delicious paella, adapted from the Valenciana type, is one of his specialties.

5 cups water
1 tsp. turmeric
1 large onion, chopped
3 chicken bouillon cubes
1 tbsp. flour
½ tsp. salt
12 to 24 chicken wings
½ cup salad oil
1 cup chopped ham or garlic sausage (optional)
1 medium onion, minced
2 cloves garlic, crushed
1 pimiento, diced
2 tomatoes, peeled and chopped
2 cups uncooked long grain rice
4 cups of prepared bouillon
1 can (5 oz.) small baby clams
½-1 pkg. frozen green peas

Boil together, uncovered, the water, turmeric, large onion and chicken bouillon cubes until reduced to 4 cups.

Place in a bag the chicken wings, flour and salt (use 2 tablespoons flour for 24 wings). Brown in the hot salad oil until crisply browned. Remove to a large casserole.

Over the chicken wings, sprinkle the ham or garlic sausage, if used.

Add the onion, garlic, pimiento and tomato to the fat remaining in the frying pan. Stir until well blended together. Add rice and stir until well mixed with the other ingredients. Add the 4 cups of reduced bouillon (do not strain), and the juice drained from the clams. Bring to a boil and simmer 5 minutes.

Break in the frozen peas, add the clams, and pour over the chicken wings. Cover and bake 30 to 40 minutes, in a 350° oven or until all liquid is absorbed and the rice well cooked. Serves 6-8.

CHICKEN LIVERS AND APPLES

A new experience in texture and flavor. I often replace the chicken livers with a pound of lamb's liver cut finger size. Nice served with parslied rice.

1 lb. chicken livers
3 tbsp. flour
1 tsp. paprika
½ tsp. each salt and pepper
⅓ cup butter or margarine
2 tbsp. brandy
1 large onion, finely chopped
4 medium apples, cored and sliced
2 tbsp. brown sugar

Clean chicken livers, cut in two. Blend flour, paprika, salt and pepper. Toss liver in mixture, until well coated.

Sauté in 4 tablespoons of the butter over high heat, until brown, stirring all the time. Pour brandy on top. Stir together and remove liver to a hot plate. To the same pan, add the onion (without any fat) and stir, over medium heat, until some of the onions are a golden color. Add to liver.

Add remaining butter to pan, add apples and sugar and stir, over medium heat, until apples start to soften, about 5 minutes. Add liver and onions to apples and toss together for a few seconds. Taste for seasoning and serve. Serves 4 to 5.

HARE EN POT

Québecois and Vermonters share many a traditional recipe and this one is an example. At the same time it has a similarity to English jugged hare. It makes a superb hot buffet casserole.

3- to 4-lb. hare, or rabbit
6 tbsp. flour
1 tsp. salt
¼ tsp. pepper
1 tsp. brown sugar

1 tsp. savory
4 tbsp. butter
5-6 slices of bacon
1 onion
3 cloves
rind 1 lemon, grated
6 peppercorns
1 bay leaf
2 tbsp. minced parsley stems
1½ cups water, or light red wine
2 tbsp. red currant jelly
garlic croutons

Cut the hare or rabbit into 6 or 8 pieces. Roll in 4 tablespoons of the flour mixed with salt, pepper, brown sugar and savory.

Brown the floured pieces in butter. Line a casserole dish with bacon slices. Place the pieces of browned hare on top.

Add the onion stuck with cloves, the grated lemon rind, peppercorns, bay leaf and minced parsley stems. Pour 1¼ cups of the water, or light red wine, on top. Do not mix.

Cover and cook in a 325° oven for 2 hours, or until the hare is tender.

Transfer hare pieces to a hot dish. Thicken the gravy with the remaining 2 tablespoons flour mixed with the remaining ¼ cup red wine or water. When the gravy is creamy, add currant jelly. Taste and add more seasoning if necessary. Pour gravy over the hare and garnish with garlic croutons. Serves 6-8.

VEGETABLES

FRESH ASPARAGUS CASSEROLE

I usually reserve the stems for this and use the tips for salad. It's perfect for a garden luncheon and, best of all, you can prepare it in the morning and refrigerate it uncooked until ready to bake.

2 tbsp. butter
1 small onion, minced
2 cups fresh mushrooms, sliced
½ tsp. curry powder
4 tbsp. flour
1 cup chicken broth
1 cup milk
½ tsp. salt
1 tsp. Worcestershire sauce
20-24 stalks cooked asparagus
2 hard-boiled eggs, sliced
½ cup bread cubes, toasted

Melt the butter in a large frying pan. Add the onion, stir over high heat for a few seconds, then add the sliced mushrooms and curry powder and keep stirring for an additional minute or two.

Lower the heat, add the flour and mix well. Mix in the chicken broth, then add the milk. Stir until smooth and creamy, then season with the salt and Worcestershire sauce.

Place the asparagus in the bottom of a generously buttered casserole. Top with the egg slices and pour the sauce over all. Sprinkle with the bread cubes and bake at 375° for 30-35 minutes. Serves 4-5.

JUNE FRESH GREEN PEAS

This is so good that I usually double the recipe and serve it as a main course for lunch, with crispy French bread and thin slices of Gouda cheese.

3 tbsp. butter
2 white onions, finely chopped
1 medium head of lettuce
2-3 lbs. unshelled green peas
½ tsp. sugar
4 sprigs parsley

Melt the butter in a 300° frypan. Add onions, cover and simmer until soft and transparent, but not brown. Reserve outer leaves of lettuce, shred rest and place on onions. Shell peas, place over lettuce and sprinkle with sugar.

Top with reserved lettuce leaves, cover and lower heat to 200°. Cook 25-35 minutes (depending on size of peas) and when done, remove lettuce leaves. Season to taste, adding a piece of butter and a bit of lemon juice, mix and garnish with parsley. Serves 6.

BEST MASHED POTATOES

Through the years, I've tried many ways of preparing mashed potatoes. These are my winners, very smooth, white and creamy. I prefer to pressure-cook my potatoes, but they can also be boiled.

8 potatoes, peeled and halved
4 tbsp. instant skim milk powder
½ to ¾ cup commercial sour cream
¼ tsp. savory
1 green onion, minced (optional)
salt and pepper, to taste

Boil the potatoes until they're tender, then drain and put pan back over heat until the potatoes are dry. Put them through a potato ricer over the cooking pan, add the remainder of the ingredients and beat until light and smooth.

Variations:
— To serve with roast pork or sausages, add 2 cups of cooked mashed turnips to the above recipe, replace the savory with sage.
— To serve with chicken, fish or eggs, add 1½ cups cooked, mashed carrots to the above and replace savory with basil.
— To serve with lamb, beef or hamburger, add 1 cup of onion, fried in bacon fat and mixed with the savory, to the above.

POTATO PANCAKES

These are delicious with any pot roast or daube. The leftover pancakes can be frozen.

6 potatoes, peeled
¼ cup breadcrumbs
2 eggs, beaten
1 onion, grated
salt and pepper, to taste
2-3 tbsp. bacon fat or lard

Grate peeled potatoes and keep in iced water to prevent their turning black. When ready to make pancakes, drain potatoes and squeeze very dry in a towel (I find a terry towel effective). Combine potatoes with breadcrumbs, beaten eggs, onion, salt and pepper.

Heat fat in a frying pan and drop potato mixture, a spoonful at a time, into pan as for pancakes. Brown on one side, turn and cook till brown on other side. Keep warm in oven. Serve with pickled red cabbage. Serves 6-8.

ELEGANT COLCANNON

I call this dish by this name because I was inspired by the Irish cabbage and potato colcannon to create a combination with carrots. I sometimes substitute turnips for the carrots, and at other times I add grated cheese, about ½ cup. It is a very nice casserole to serve with roast turkey or chicken.

4 to 6 carrots, peeled and cubed
3 medium-sized potatoes, pared and cubed
1 medium-sized onion, sliced
⅛ tsp. dried thyme or
½ tsp. dried basil
3 tbsp. butter
milk or water (about ⅔ cup)
1 egg
¼ cup commercial sour cream
salt and pepper
¼ cup chopped parsley

Place in a saucepan the carrots, potatoes, onion, thyme or basil, and 1 tablespoon of the butter. Add enough water or milk to cover 1 inch of the bottom. Cover and simmer until the vegetables are tender. This should take 10 to 15 minutes.

If you have a blender, pour in the drained vegetables and add just enough of the cooking liquid to make a thick purée; or make a purée by pressing the vegetables through a food mill or sieve.

To the hot purée, add the egg, sour cream, and the remaining butter. Add salt and pepper to taste. Whip over low heat until creamy and fluffy. Serve sprinkled with parsley. Serves 4-6.

NEW POTATOES IN CUCUMBER SAUCE

To make this ahead of time, cook and peel the potatoes, prepare dressing, cover and keep both at room temperature. Then they can be combined in a matter of seconds before heating.

18-24 small new potatoes
5-6 green onions, finely chopped
1 medium cucumber, unpeeled
juice of 1 lemon
1 tsp. salt
½ tsp. paprika
4 tbsp. mayonnaise

Cook the whole potatoes in their skins, drain and dry a few seconds over the heat. Let cool slightly and peel, cutting any large ones into thick slices. Mix in onions and set aside.

Grate the cucumber on a fine grater, removing all seeds. Place in top of a double boiler with remaining ingredients and stir over boiling water until well blended. Add potatoes and stir gently over simmering water until hot. Serves 10.

FRITTATA

The best Frittata is made in Genoa, where any combination of vegetables may be used. I like mine best when the vegetables are cooked in a shallow ceramic baking dish and the eggs are poured on top.

1 tbsp. salad oil
½ tbsp. butter
1 onion, thinly sliced
1 green pepper, diced
1 zucchini (small Italian squash)
6-8 beet tops or spinach leaves, coarsely chopped *or*
1 peeled tomato, diced
1 tbsp. water
½ tsp. sugar
6 eggs
3 tsp. cold water
Parmesan cheese, grated

Heat together the oil and butter, add the onion and cook until soft and lightly browned. Add the green pepper and stir a few seconds with the onions. Slice the unpeeled zucchini and add to the green pepper with the beet tops, spinach leaves or tomatoes. Add the 1 tbsp. water and the sugar. Cover and simmer 5 minutes over low heat.

Prepare the omelette mixture. Salt and pepper the vegetables to taste, pour the omelette on top and cook. Do not turn or fold. Slide the omelette onto a hot platter and serve with the grated cheese. Serves 6.

LEMON NUTMEG CARROTS

These are one of my summer favorites. I cook the carrots, make the sauce, and refrigerate both until they're needed. Then only a few minutes are required to combine and warm the two before dinner.

12 young carrots
a pinch of sugar
salt to taste
1½ tsp. boiling water
2 tbsp. butter
1 tbsp. fresh lemon juice
⅛ tsp. nutmeg

Wash and scrape the carrots and place in a saucepan. Add a pinch of sugar, then pour boiling water on top. Cover and boil 10-15 minutes, depending on the size of the carrots—keep them crisp. Drain. Salt to taste and refrigerate.

Mix the rest of the ingredients and refrigerate.

To serve, simmer the two together over low heat for 3-5 minutes, then sprinkle with parsley. Serves 6.

TOMATO SCALLOP

A tasty casserole that follows the weather, this can be served hot on cold days, and vice versa. It's a good traveller, but you can also take the ingredients you need and quickly put them together at the cottage. Serve it with cold cuts or barbecued chicken.

19-oz. can tomatoes
1 onion, chopped
1 tbsp. sugar
½ tsp. salt
¼ tsp. oregano
dash of rosemary
1 cup bread, cut in ½-inch cubes
⅓ cup grated mild Cheddar cheese

Combine tomatoes, onion, sugar and seasonings; top with bread cubes and grated cheese. Bake in 350° oven until bread cubes are browned, about 15-18 minutes. Serves 4-6.

JULIENNE OF VEGETABLES

Since any combination of vegetables can be used, this type of dish allows a lot of liberty. The important part is the cutting—it should be consistent so that all are cooked in the same time.

5 medium carrots
5 celery stalks
2 medium onions
2 parsnips or ½ a turnip
1 leek (optional)
4 tbsp. butter
½ tsp. thyme
juice of ½ a lemon

Peel the vegetables and cut into match-like shreds. Melt butter in a saucepan just large enough to hold vegetables, add them to pan with 2 tbsp. of water, the thyme, and salt and pepper to taste. Cover tightly and simmer over low heat 20-35 minutes, or until tender. Add lemon juice and taste for seasoning. Serves 10.

IRENE'S CREAMED MUSHROOMS

The onion browns in a heavy metal pan without any fat. It is an intriguing way to deal with onions, they retain all their fine flavor with none of the harshness.

1 onion, chopped fine
½ lb. fresh mushrooms, sliced
⅓ cup cold water
2 tbsp. butter
2 tbsp. flour
½ cup sour cream
salt and pepper to taste

Place the onion in a heavy metal frying pan without any fat. Cook over medium heat, until lightly browned. Add the mushrooms, mix well and stir together for a few minutes, add the water, simmer 10 minutes.

In the meantime, brown the butter in a saucepan, add the flour and brown together, add the liquid from the mushrooms, cook, while stirring, until creamy and smooth. Pour over the mushrooms. Blend well together and add the sour cream. Heat, but do not boil. Taste for seasoning and serve. Serves 4 to 6.

CUCUMBER MIZERIA

The season should not go by without summer cucumbers in this tasty, creamy sauce being served at least once. This recipe is Ukrainian.

3 medium cucumbers
1 tsp. salt
4-5 chopped green onions
1 tbsp. minced fresh dill
3 tbsp. white vinegar
½ tsp. salt
½ tsp. sugar
¼ tsp. pepper
¼ cup sour cream

Peel the cucumbers, but if they are young and freshly gathered, just wash them. Peeled or unpeeled, run a fork down their length to make parallel grooves which create an attractive scalloped edge. Then slice them as thinly as possible.

Place them on a dish, sprinkle over the salt and let stand for 15 minutes. Drain, press out the water that has accumulated, and place the slices in a bowl.

Add the onions, dill, vinegar, salt, sugar and pepper. Toss well and refrigerate for 1 hour, or just let stand for 5 minutes. Spread the sour cream on top just before serving. A sprig of dill placed on top of the sour cream looks very nice. Serves 4-6.

DUTCH COLESLAW

If you are going to give a harvest party, consider serving a large, cold boiled ham, hot boiled potatoes and this Dutch Coleslaw. A big jar of good mustard, apple dumplings and cider will make the meal perfect.

4-5 cups thinly sliced cabbage
2 diced celery stalks
2 thinly sliced onions
4 grated carrots, in medium shreds
2 tbsp. sugar
½ cup rich cream
2 tbsp. cider vinegar
½-1 tsp. salt
¼ tsp. pepper
¼ cup minced fresh parsley

Combine the cabbage, celery, onions and carrots. Place them in a large bowl and completely cover with ice water. Refrigerate for 1 hour, then drain thoroughly.

Combine the sugar, cream, vinegar, salt and pepper (the vinegar will thicken the cream). Pour over the vegetables when ready to serve and toss very well. Sprinkle the minced parsley on top. Serves 6.

OLD-FASHIONED POTATO SALAD

This potato salad has perfect keeping quality, and is most tasty. The cooked dressing is my grand-mère's. My mother taught me how to make the salad, and the oil dressing is my recipe.

5-6 cups cooked potatoes, diced
1 tsp. salt
¼ tsp. pepper, freshly ground
¼ tsp. dry mustard
generous pinch of tarragon
pinch of garlic powder (optional)
1 tbsp. fresh lemon juice
3 tbsp. salad oil
1 cup celery, diced
crisp lettuce or watercress

Place the diced potatoes in a large bowl. Shake the salt, pepper, dry mustard, tarragon, garlic powder, lemon juice and salad oil together in a bottle.

Pour over the potatoes, toss gently and cover the bowl. Let stand for 2 hours but do not refrigerate.

When ready to serve, add the celery and ½ cup or so of grand-mère's cooked dressing. Mix lightly and serve in a nest of lettuce or watercress. Serves 6-8.

POTATO "CIVETTE"

A fantastic sort of potato salad, created by a French épicure friend of mine who says it refreshes the palate and enhances the fineness of the meat. I can vouch for the truth of this. Serve it in a black ebony bowl or in gleaming cut glass as the French do.

16 to 20 small potatoes
¼ cup chives or green onion tops, chopped fine
1 tsp. sugar
¼ tsp. freshly ground pepper
½ tsp. salt
2 tbsp. olive oil
juice of 2 lemons

Make sure the potatoes are the same size.

Peel a little band, about an inch wide, around the middle of each scrubbed potato.

Place the potatoes in a steamer (the sort of double boiler with the bottom of its top piece perforated) or in a sieve or colander that can rest on the rim of a pot of boiling water, but well above the water, as the potatoes are steamed, not boiled. Cover pan with cover or foil.

Steam 20 to 30 minutes or until potatoes are tender. Turn onto a folded cloth and let them cool, until they can be handled, then remove peel which almost comes off by itself.

Prepare the dressing while the potatoes cool. Place in a mortar or in a bowl the chives or green onions, sugar, pepper and salt. Crush this to a paste with the pestle or a wooden spoon, slowly adding the oil and lemon juice alternately. Then stir about 5 minutes until mixture turns sort of creamy. Pour over the potatoes, stir until well mixed. They will take on a lime green color. Set in serving dish. Sprinkle lightly with paprika. Cover with wax paper and keep at room temperature until ready to use. Serves 8.

TYROLIAN TOMATOES

Prepare this cooked salad with the beautiful color a day or so ahead of time. Surrounded with a crown of crisp watercress, it looks very dramatic presented in individual French porcelain ramekins or a smart Copenhagen blue serving dish.

> ½ lb. fresh mushrooms (see below)
> 4 tbsp. olive oil
> 1 large onion, finely chopped
> 2 garlic cloves, finely chopped
> ¼ cup vinegar (red wine or cider)
> 1 tsp. sugar
> 4-6 peeled tomatoes, chopped
> ¼ tsp. thyme
> 1 crushed bay leaf
> 2 tbsp. finely chopped parsley

Use button mushrooms if possible, removing stems and leaving caps whole. If not available, remove stems from ordinary mushrooms and slice caps. Heat 3 tbsp. of the oil in a frying pan, stir mushroom caps over high heat for 3 minutes and set aside.

Heat remaining oil in a saucepan, add onion, garlic, and stir constantly over medium heat until lightly browned. Add vinegar, sugar, and boil uncovered over medium heat until reduced by half. Add tomatoes, thyme, bay leaf, parsley, and simmer uncovered over low heat 30 minutes.

Add mushrooms, stir thoroughly and pour into a dish. Let cool and, when tepid, add salt and pepper to taste. Cover and refrigerate until needed. I fill my ramekins in the morning and refrigerate them until 1 hour before serving. Serves 4-6.

TOMATO-CUCUMBER SALAD

My family's favorite whenever we have an outdoor charcoal-broiled feast.

4 tomatoes, sliced
¼ cup salad oil
¼ cup cider or red wine vinegar
1 tbsp. parsley, chopped
dill, fresh or dried, to taste
3 green onions, finely chopped
small head of lettuce
2 cucumbers, peeled and sliced
salt and pepper, to taste

Place the tomatoes in a bowl with the oil, vinegar, parsley, dill and onions. Refrigerate 1 to 2 hours. When ready to serve, shred the lettuce as you would a cabbage, add to tomatoes with the cucumbers, salt and pepper. Toss lightly until well blended. Serves 4.

ORANGE AND PIMIENTO SALAD

A wonderfully colorful salad, this teams a fruit and vegetable in a very unusual combination.

6 large oranges
6 red sweet peppers
5 tbsp. salad oil
3 tbsp. wine vinegar
1 tsp. Dijon mustard
salt, to taste

Place oranges in a large bowl of boiling water, leave 15 minutes, then drain. Peel when cool enough, removing all cellulose (the white inner skin) and slice thinly.

Remove cores, seeds and membranes from washed peppers and cut into julienne strips. Thoroughly beat remaining ingredients.

Place alternate layers of oranges and peppers in a bowl, sprinkling each layer with the dressing. Chill and, just before serving, stir gently. Serves 6.

PASTA AND RICE

MEATLESS LASAGNE

My daughter's large recipe to serve 10. Make in one dish or prepare 2 casseroles, serve one, freeze the other for emergency.

20 cups water
1 tbsp. each salt and salad oil
1 lb. (16 oz.) lasagne noodles
2 lbs. cottage cheese
1 cup commercial sour cream
2 eggs
½ tsp. pepper
½ tsp. oregano
1 lb. Mozzarella cheese, thinly sliced
3 tbsp. salad oil
2 large onions, chopped fine
¼ cup celery, chopped fine
1 (28-oz.) can tomatoes
2 (6-oz.) cans tomato paste
¼ tsp. pepper
1 tsp. basil
2 tsp. sugar
2 (4-oz.) cans chopped mushrooms
or
1½ lbs. ground beef

Bring water to boil in soup kettle. Add the salt and salad oil. Then add the lasagne noodles, one by one, boil 10 to 15 minutes or until tender. When done pour cold water into the pot until noodles are cold enough to be handled, but do not drain.

While the lasagne cooks and cools prepare the following.

Mix the cottage cheese, sour cream, eggs, pepper and oregano, salt to taste. Butter a large oblong dish or 28-inch casserole.

Set the sliced Mozzarella ready to be used.

Make the mushroom sauce. Heat 2 tablespoons of the oil in large frying pan, add the onions and celery, stir until lightly browned. Strain tomatoes to remove seeds, pressing down the pulp. Add to onions, add tomato paste, pepper, basil, sugar. Boil 10 minutes.

Heat remaining tablespoon of oil. Add the drained mushrooms. Stir until hot. Add to sauce. Taste for seasoning. Then assemble casserole in a large baking dish or divide in 2 casseroles. Place a layer of noodles in long strips to cover the bottom. Next, a layer of creamed cheese mixture, then slices of Mozzarella, then mushroom sauce. Repeat these layers until dish is filled, ending with noodles, sauce and topping of sliced cheese.

Bake either size in a preheated 325° oven for 1½ hours. Refrigerate or freeze, covered, without baking. To serve, bake at 350° for 1½ hours. Serves 10.

MY NOODLE CASSEROLE

When I can't think of what to cook for a light meal, I often prepare this simple casserole. We never find it dull.

8 oz. noodles
1¼ cups plain yogurt or sour cream
8 oz. cottage cheese
¼ cup butter or margarine
½ tsp. salt
¼ tsp. pepper
4 tbsp. chopped parsley
3 green onions, chopped (optional)
1 egg, lightly beaten

Cook noodles according to package directions, then drain. Put back into pan with remaining ingredients and stir with a fork over low heat until heated through. Pour into a 1½-quart casserole (you can prepare this ahead of time) and bake uncovered in a 300° oven 45 minutes. Serves 6.

CHEDDAR BAKED MACARONI

The personality of this baked macaroni is in the combination of grated and diced cheddar. Please use strong old cheddar. The tossed breadcrumbs on top can be covered with an additional ½ cup of diced cheddar or Swiss cheese.

16 oz. elbow macaroni
1 cup grated cheddar cheese
1 cup diced cheddar cheese
3 tbsp. butter
½ cup celery, cut in small dice
1 onion, minced
4 tbsp. flour
2 cups milk
1 cup light cream
salt and pepper to taste
½ cup dry breadcrumbs
1 tbsp. melted butter

Cook according to directions on package, drain and place half the macaroni in a buttered baking dish. Sprinkle with half of the grated and half the diced cheese. Add the rest of the macaroni and cover with the rest of the cheese.

Melt the butter, add the celery and onion, simmer 10 minutes over low heat. Add the flour, mix, then add the milk and cream, cook until creamy. Salt and pepper to taste. Pour over the macaroni. Toss the breadcrumbs with the melted butter and sprinkle over the macaroni. Bake 40 minutes, uncovered, in a 350° oven. Serves 6.

THE EASIEST OF ALL TOMATO MACARONI

I have had so many requests for this quickly prepared recipe that it is a pleasure to pass it on to you. It is equally good hot or cold. Cold, I like to serve it with thinly sliced cold roast beef or a green salad.

20-oz. can tomatoes
1 tbsp. sugar
1 tsp. dry mustard
½ tsp. pepper
¼ tsp. thyme or ½ tsp. savory
¼-½ cup celery leaves, finely chopped
1 tsp. paprika
6-oz. can tomato paste
½ lb. macaroni, cooked
½ lb. cheese, grated
breadcrumbs
butter

Pour ⅓ of the canned tomatoes into a well-buttered casserole or baking dish. To the remaining tomatoes add the sugar, dry mustard, pepper, thyme or savory, celery leaves, paprika and tomato paste. Mix together thoroughly.

Make alternate layers of the tomato mixture, macaroni and grated cheese, sprinkle with breadcrumbs and dot with butter. Bake in a 350° oven for 35-45 minutes. Serves 6.

RED WINE SPAGHETTI SAUCE

Chianti is, of course, the best choice for a spaghetti sauce, but any other type of red wine will do. This sauce is the specialty of the Piedmont district in Italy and it's the dried mushrooms that give it its special European flavor. They're available at specialty shops and in some gourmet departments.

2 tbsp. dried mushrooms
1 cup boiling water
1 lb. veal, in one piece
1 tsp. paprika
2 tbsp. salad oil
2 cans tomato sauce, 8-oz. each
4 large onions, sliced
½ cup dry red wine
1 tsp. basil
1 garlic clove
½ tsp. sugar

Cover mushrooms with a cupful of boiling water and let them soak 1 hour.

Sprinkle veal with paprika and brown in the salad oil over medium heat. Reserving ¼ cup of tomato sauce, add remainder to pan with rest of ingredients, including mushroom water. Salt and pepper to taste and bring to a boil. Cover and simmer until meat is tender, about 1 hour.

Remove meat from sauce, let cool, then chop it finely with a sharp knife (if you put it through a meat chopper, you'll lose too much juice). Return meat to sauce, add reserved tomato sauce and stir until well mixed and hot (but do not boil). Taste for seasoning and serve over pasta of your choice. This sauce is even better made in advance and reheated; it freezes well. Yield: 4-4½ cups.

ITALIAN CHEESE LOAF

This most versatile cheese loaf can be served hot or allowed to cool and sliced like bread or cut into 2-inch squares and fried in butter or bacon fat and served with bacon.

1 cup uncooked short grain rice
4 eggs
6 tbsp. salad oil
½ tsp. basil
¼ cup minced parsley
1 cup grated strong or mild cheese
salt and pepper to taste

Cook the rice according to directions on package.

Beat 3 of the eggs with rotary beater, add salad oil and beat well. To this, add the remaining ingredients and the cooked rice.

Oil a 6" x 10" loaf pan. Pour in mixture spreading it evenly on top and cover with the well-beaten remaining egg. Bake in a 350° oven for 30 minutes. Good served with a tomato sauce. Serves 6.

WILD RICE A LA FERGUSON

Nowadays, 1 cup or ½ cup wild rice should make a main course for 6, because of its cost.

1 cup wild rice
3 tbsp. butter
1 small onion, minced
2 stalks celery, diced
½ cup fresh parsley, minced
¼ tsp. thyme
3 medium carrots, grated
½ lb. strong Cheddar cheese, grated
1½ cups chicken stock
2 tbsp. butter, diced

Wash the rice under running water and spread on a towel to dry for 2 hours.

Melt the 3 tablespoons butter in a heavy frying pan. Brown the onions until tender. Remove from frying pan and add the dry wild rice to the remaining butter. Cook stirring constantly, until a hazelnut fragrance emanates from the rice.

Mix together the celery, parsley, thyme, carrots and browned onions. Butter a baking dish, fill with alternate layers of wild rice, vegetables and grated cheese, until all the ingredients have been used. Cover with the chicken stock. Dot with butter.

Cover and bake in a 350° oven for 1 hour.

RICE "PARISIEN"

When in Paris in the Spring, you will find this "riz blanc" served as a lunch specialty garnished with watercress or green salad.

1 cup uncooked long grain rice
3 tbsp. butter
½ lb. cottage cheese
½ cup sour cream (commercial)
4 green onions, finely minced
minced parsley, to taste
salt and pepper, to taste

Cook the rice according to directions on package.

Melt the butter in a saucepan. Add the cooked rice, cottage cheese, sour cream, green onions, parsley, salt and pepper. Stir together with a fork. Cover.

Cook over very low heat about 15 minutes or just enough to warm thoroughly, stirring once or twice during the cooking period. Serves 6.

GOLDEN RICE SPINACH CASSEROLE

My favorite vegetable casserole with hot baked ham. Also very nice topped with 4 to 6 sliced hard-cooked eggs, served as a main course.

⅓ cup salad oil
1 tbsp. turmeric
¼ tsp. aniseed (optional)
1 onion, chopped fine
1 cup uncooked short grain rice
2 cups boiling water
1¼ tsp. salt
1 bag fresh spinach
6 green onions, chopped fine
¼ cup fresh dill or parsley, chopped

Heat the salad oil, add the turmeric and aniseed. Stir quickly over high heat until they are quite hot. Add the onion and the rice, stir a few minutes or until well blended; lower the heat and cook 10 minutes, stirring often.

Add the boiling water and salt. Bring to a fast boil. Cover and simmer 15 minutes.

Wash and chop the spinach rather coarsely. Slice the green onions, mix the spinach, onion, dill or parsley.

Make alternate rows of cooked rice and raw mixed greens, in a buttered casserole. Salt and pepper each row lightly. Top with a few dots of butter. Cover and bake 30 minutes in a 350° oven. Serves 6.

SUMMER RICE SALAD

For a change serve this light colorful salad to replace the usual potato salad.

Place all the ingredients in the blender jar and almost fill it with water. Cover and blend for 3 minutes at high speed. Pass the mixture through a coarse strainer, then add more water to taste. Serve very cold or over ice.

The straining is not absolutely necessary—the small specks of lemon and celery leaves are pleasant to munch. Serves 7-9.

SUNSHINE CUP

An electric blender is a must for this superb natural beverage. To the dieters you invite for lunch, serve a tall glass of this with a green salad or a plate of crunchy raw vegetables and a small bowl of unsalted nuts.

½ cup diced carrots, unpeeled
1 celery stalk, diced
½ an unpeeled cucumber, sliced
½ cup fresh orange juice
1 tsp. fresh lime juice (optional)
1 tbsp. raw or brown sugar
1 slice unpeeled lemon
pinch of sea salt or salt

Place the carrots and 1 cup of water in a blender jar. Cover and blend about 2 minutes at high speed until carrots are liquified. Still blending, carefully add remaining ingredients. Blend 2 minutes and serve with or without ice. Serves 1.

DESSERTS

CREAM OF LIQUEUR

A smart, delectable, miniature dessert with a sophisticated topping of slivered toasted almonds. It gleams in small oriental dessert dishes, and should be accompanied by a bottle of the same liqueur chosen to make it, a liqueur glass with each dessert, not to sip but to use as a measure to pour over the dessert. It makes a befitting ending to a perfect meal.

1¼ cups light cream
1½ envelopes of unflavored gelatine
3 egg yolks
½ cup sugar
a pinch of salt
⅓ cup liqueur of your choice*
3 egg whites
⅓ cup slivered almonds

Measure the cream in a saucepan. Add the gelatine, let stand 5 minutes. Then stir over low heat, until gelatine is melted. Beat the egg yolks with the sugar and salt. Add to the hot milk, stir together 5 or 6 minutes. Remove from heat, stir in the liqueur.

Beat the egg whites until stiff and fold into the gelatine mixture. When well mixed, pour into individual dishes. Refrigerate at least 4 hours, or overnight.

Place the slivered almonds on a baking sheet and set in a 325° oven until toasted, about 20 minutes. Cool, set aside. Sprinkle to taste over each dish of cream when ready to serve. Serves 8.

Benedictine, B and B, Cointreau, Kalua Coffee liqueur, Crème de Menthe, rum, brandy or bourbon are all equally nice. Each one gives the dessert a different flavor.

SOUR CREAM CHOCOLATE CAKE

A self-frosted, one-layer cake that is both attractive and easy to put together.

6 tbsp. soft butter or margarine
1 cup sugar
2 eggs, at room temperature
1⅓ cups all-purpose flour
1½ tsp. baking powder
1 tsp. each soda and cinnamon
1 cup commercial sour cream
6-oz. package semi-sweet chocolate chips

Place the butter, sugar and eggs in the bowl of an electric mixer and beat at medium speed 10 minutes. Sift dry ingredients together and blend by hand into creamed mixture. Mix sour cream in well.

Pour batter into a greased and flour-dusted 9 x 13-inch baking pan. Scatter the chocolate chips evenly over top, then sprinkle with a tablespoonful of sugar.

Bake in a 350° oven 35 minutes, or until cake just begins to pull away from sides of pan. Let cool in the pan on a cake rack and keep at room temperature. To serve, cut into small rectangles or squares. Yield: 50-60 squares 1½ x 1½ inches.

GLAZED CARROT NUT CAKE

This will keep for three months in the freezer, and I always like to have one on hand. If you don't want to make the orange glaze, simply put whipped cream on the cake when you are ready to serve.

1¼ cups salad oil
2 cups fine granulated sugar
2 cups all-purpose flour
2 tsp. baking powder
1 tsp. each soda and salt
2 tsp. cinnamon
4 eggs
3 cups grated raw carrots
1 cup finely chopped walnuts or pecans
glaze (see below)

Beat the oil and sugar with an electric mixer at medium speed for 5 minutes. Sift the next 5 dry ingredients together and stir half into sugar mixture. Blend thoroughly. Add remaining half of dry ingredients alternately with eggs, one at a time, mixing well after each addition. Add carrots and nuts, mix well 'and pour into a lightly oiled 10-inch tube pan. Bake in a 325° oven 1¼ hours. Remove from oven, invert on a cake rack, unmold and let cool.

For the glaze: place in a saucepan 1 cup of sugar, grated peel of ½ an orange, ¼ cup of cornstarch and 1 cup of fresh orange juice. Stir until well mixed, then add 1 tsp. of lemon juice, 2 tbsp. of butter and ½ tsp. of salt. Cook over medium low heat, stirring until thick and glossy, about 3-5 minutes. Let cool until tepid, then spread on unmolded cake. When cool, freeze cake on a tray, then remove cake, wrap, label and put back in freezer.

COFFEE CHARLOTTE RUSSE

In Victorian days, no dinner for guests was complete without its Charlotte Russe. To vary the dessert, use the flavoring of your choice (vanilla, rum, brandy, rose water) in equal quantity to replace the modern touch of instant coffee.

½ cup sugar
1 envelope unflavored gelatin
⅛ tsp. salt
2 tbsp. instant coffee
1¼ cups milk
2 eggs, separated
½ tsp. vanilla
1 cup whipping cream
8-12 ladyfingers

Mix together ¼ cup of the sugar, gelatin, salt and instant coffee in the top of a double boiler. Beat the milk with the egg yolks and add to the gelatin mixture. Cook over boiling water, stirring constantly, for 5 minutes or until the gelatin is dissolved. Remove from heat, add the vanilla and refrigerate until the mixture is half set.

Beat the egg whites, add the remaining ¼ cup of sugar and beat until peaks form. Fold the half-set coffee mixture into the stiff egg whites. Whip the cream and add to the coffee mixture.

Set the ladyfingers in individual molds or in a crystal bowl, pour in the cream and refrigerate 4-12 hours. Serves 8.

HOT BREAD APPLE CHARLOTTE

This "Charlotte" is a family version of the rich, crusty, French classique. A must is to serve it hot, with a lavish amount of sweetened whipped cream flavored with a few drops of almond extract.

The dough base:

1 cup flour
½ tsp. baking powder
¼ tsp. salt
2 tbsp. sugar
3 tbsp. soft butter
2 eggs, beaten
2-3 tbsp. milk

Filling:

5 cups sliced peeled apples
½ cup seedless raisins
1 cup apple juice
¼ cup rum
⅔ cup sugar
1 tsp. cinnamon
grated rind of ½ lemon

To make the dough, sift together the flour, baking powder, salt and sugar. Cut in the butter and work in smoothly with a wooden spoon. Beat in the eggs. Stir in the milk, the dough must be stiff yet somewhat soft, and so use discretion in the amount of milk needed.

Grease an 8-inch spring form pan. With rubber spatula or spoon, spread dough on the bottom and part way up the sides of the pan. The top edge will look ragged.

Prepare the filling: Place in saucepan the apple slices, raisins and apple juice. Cook, uncovered, over medium heat, until the apples are soft, but have not lost their shape. Strain over a bowl. Place liquid back in the saucepan, add the rum and boil until syrupy. Set aside.

Combine the sugar, cinnamon and lemon ring, stir gently into the apple-raisin mixture. Spoon into the dough-lined pan. Bake in preheated 425° oven 50 to 60 minutes or until crust is deep golden brown and filling is firm. Cool 10 minutes. Open spring mold and slide "Charlotte" on plate. Warm up rum syrup and pour all over dough and apples. Serves 6.

CARAMEL BREAD PUDDING

I consider this my best bread pudding.

¾ cup brown sugar
1 egg, beaten
2 slices heavily buttered bread
1½ cups milk
1 tsp. vanilla

Pack sugar in a buttered casserole, cut bread in small pieces and place buttered side down on sugar. Mix egg, milk and vanilla and pour over mixture. Put in oven and bake until nicely browned. Serve with or without cream. Serves 4.

MACAROON RICE PUDDING

This scrumptious rice pudding with its almond macaroon crusted top is equally delicious hot or cold. Serve as is or with table cream or whipped cream.

4 cups milk
½ cup sugar
⅓ cup uncooked short grain rice
pinch salt
2 tbsp. soft butter
enough almond macaroons to cover top
1 egg beaten
½ tsp. vanilla
½ tsp. almond essence

Place in buttered 1½-quart casserole the milk, sugar, rice, salt and butter.

Bake uncovered, in 325° oven for 1½ hours, stirring 4 to 5 times during cooking period.

Remove from oven, cover top with macaroons, rounded side up. Beat egg with vanilla and almond essence, pour over macaroons and bake another half hour. Serves 6.

LEMON RICE CREAM

Creamy, tasty, easy to make, this rice cream will keep 4 to 6 days, well covered, in refrigerator.

1 cup uncooked short grain rice
4 cups milk
a pinch of salt
3 pieces rind cut from lemon
4 tbsp. sugar
cinnamon or nutmeg

Place all the ingredients except the cinnamon or nutmeg in a heavy metal saucepan.

Cook, uncovered, over low heat, for 1 hour. Stir a few times during the cooking period.

Pour into serving dish. Sprinkle with cinnamon or nutmeg. Cover and refrigerate until cold. Serve as is or with raspberry jam or thawed out frozen strawberries.

RED WINE JELLY

A cool colorful dessert to be made a day or so ahead and served as is, or surrounded with sweetened berries, or topped with strawberry ice cream.

2 tbsp. unflavored gelatine
¼ cup cold water
2 slices lemon peel
1 cup boiling water
½ cup sugar
1 cup gooseberry jelly
1 cup dry red wine
2 tbsp. brandy or lemon juice

Soak the gelatine in the cold water 5 minutes. In a saucepan, simmer lemon peel, boiling water, sugar and jelly over low heat until sugar and jelly are dissolved.

Add gelatine, stir to dissolve, then put mixture through a sieve. Add remaining ingredients, pour into individual molds or a 1-quart one and refrigerate. Serves 6.

FRUIT COMPOTES

Strawberry Compotes

Wash and hull 1 quart of strawberries. Place in a bowl and dribble ¼-½ cup of honey over them. Add the grated peel and juice of ½ an orange. Stir gently with your fingertips, cover and refrigerate.

Raspberry Chantilly Compote

Thaw a 10-oz. pkg. of frozen raspberries, then mash with a fork or in a blender. Put through a sieve to remove seeds. Clean 1 quart of fresh raspberries. Whip 1½ cups of whipping cream, flavor with 2 tbsp. of icing sugar, and 3 tbsp. of brandy or 2 tsp. of vanilla.

Pile the cream in the centre of a glass dish, surround with fresh raspberries and gently spread raspberry purée over berries. Serve with a basket of hot biscuits, each guest pouring the compote over the biscuits.

Black Cherry Burgundy Compote

Stem and pit 1 lb. of large B.C. Bing cherries. Place in a pan with ¼ cup of honey and ¼ cup of red Burgundy or port. Cook over low heat until red juice oozes out of the cherries. Stir in 2 tbsp. of cornstarch, and the juice of ½ an orange or 3 tbsp. of rum. Keep stirring until mixture is creamy and transparent and serve hot or cold with hot biscuits.

Superb Peach Berry Compote

Peel and slice enough fresh peaches to fill an 8-oz. measuring cup. Pour them into a serving dish and do the same with an equal quantity of hulled fresh strawberries or blueberries. Mash contents of two 1-pint baskets of raspberries with 3 tbsp. of icing sugar and pour over fruit in bowl. Sprinkle generously with icing sugar, cover and refrigerate. The mixture is stirred only when you're ready to pour it over the biscuits. Yield: 3-4 cups.

Blueberry or Currant Compote

Stem, wash and dry 4 cups of blueberries or currants and place in a serving dish. Combine ¼ cup of corn syrup, 1 tbsp. of grated orange peel, ¼ cup of fresh orange juice and bring to a boil. Simmer over low heat 3 minutes, then stir in 3 tbsp. of honey and pour over fruit. Cover and let stand at room temperature and, when cool, refrigerate. If you wish, add 3 tbsp. of orange liqueur or brandy before serving. Yield: 3-4 cups.

TANGERINE COMPOTE

This will freeze well for up to 5 months at 0°. Give it 4-6 hours of thawing before you serve it.

2 navel oranges
6 tangerines
½ cup honey
1 cup fresh orange juice
grated peel of 1 orange
3 tbsp. orange liqueur (optional)

Peel the oranges and slice them paper-thin. Peel tangerines and break into sections. Put them in a bowl in alternating layers, sprinkling each with a dribble of honey.

Boil orange juice with peel 15 minutes over medium-low heat. Let cool, add liqueur and pour over fruit. Cover and refrigerate. Serves 4-6.

PORTUGUESE SWEET

They refer to this easy sweet as "Rapido". It is all of that and very pleasant as well.

6-8 tangerines
8 tbsp. bitter marmalade
3 tbsp. rum or tangerine juice
grated unsweetened chocolate

Peel tangerines, break into sections and place in a dish. Boil marmalade and rum or juice over medium heat 2 minutes, pour over fruit sections, cover and refrigerate. Serve topped with as much grated chocolate as you like. Serves 4-5.

FRESH STRAWBERRY PIE GLACE

The "glacé" is the French way of flavoring the fresh fruit pie without cooking the berries. It is beautiful to look at and very fragrant with the strawberry flavor.

4 cups fresh strawberries
1 cup sugar
1 tbsp. cornstarch
1 tsp. grated lemon peel
1 tbsp. lemon juice
10-inch pie shell, baked

Crush 1½ cups of the strawberries with a fork, add the sugar, cornstarch, lemon peel and juice. Stir together until well blended. Cook over medium heat until transparent, stirring most of the time.

Fill the baked shell with the rest of the strawberries, placing them point up. Pour over the hot berry syrup, which should cover them completely with a shiny topping—the "glacé". Chill and serve. Serves 6-8.

STRAWBERRY-RHUBARB COBBLER

What an affinity there is between strawberries and rhubarb: this superb pudding would not be nearly as good made with just the strawberries or rhubarb alone.

1½ cups sugar
1 cup apple juice
½ cup water
2 cups diced rhubarb
2 cups sliced strawberries
1 tsp. vanilla
1 cup all-purpose flour
2 tbsp. sugar
1½ tsp. baking powder
½ tsp. mace
¼ cup butter
¼ cup milk or cream
sugar and nutmeg
soft butter

Bring the sugar, apple juice and water to a boil and stir until sugar is dissolved. Remove from heat, add the rhubarb, strawberries and vanilla. Mix well and pour into a pudding dish.

To prepare the batter, sift together the flour, sugar, baking powder and mace. Cut in the butter and add the milk or cream.

Stir quickly to blend, and drop by spoonfuls over the fruit. Sprinkle top with sugar and a dash of nutmeg, and brush with soft butter. Bake at 450° for 20-25 minutes. Serves 6.

STRAWBERRIES NEVERS

I have a friend who sends me a jar of superb homemade Seville orange marmalade every year. I keep it to make this dessert. The preparation is simplicity itself and the result is luscious.

1 qt. fresh strawberries
1 cup Seville orange marmalade
¼ cup orange-flavored liqueur, or brandy
½ cup fresh orange juice
1 tsp. grated orange rind
1 tsp. lemon juice
whipped cream (optional)

Wash strawberries before hulling them. Drain thoroughly on an absorbent towel. Hull.

Mix marmalade with liqueur or brandy over low heat and stir until well blended. Add orange juice gradually, while stirring, until enough is used to give a medium-thick sauce. Add orange rind and lemon juice.

Put the strawberries in a cut-glass dish and pour the cooled marmalade sauce over them. Refrigerate for at least 2 hours before serving.

Serve with a bowl of whipped cream sweetened with a little marmalade and flavored with orange-flavored liqueur or brandy. It is good without the cream, too. Serves 6-8.

STRAWBERRY RHUBARB COMPOTE

I would need many superlatives to describe this early summer delight. Serve it in a glass dish with a bowl of whipped, sour, or ice cream.

½ cup orange juice
¾ cup sugar
2 lbs. rhubarb, in 2-inch pieces
1 pint fresh strawberries or
10-oz. pkg. frozen strawberries

Bring the orange juice and sugar to a boil, then stir until sugar is dissolved. Add rhubarb, simmer over low heat 5 minutes and remove from heat.

Stir in fresh (cleaned and halved) or frozen strawberries (the hot mixture will thaw them), then refrigerate. Serves 4.

BUTTER DIPPED BISCUITS

These are rich and relatively expensive, but utterly scrumptious when served piping hot, topped with a cold berry compote. This recipe can easily be cut in half.

1 cup butter or margarine
4 cups all-purpose flour
1 tsp. salt
½ cup sugar
5 tsp. baking powder
4 large eggs
1 cup milk

Put the butter in a jelly roll pan and warm in a 450° oven until melted. Sift together the flour, salt, sugar and baking powder. Stir together the eggs and milk. Pour egg mixture over the dry ingredients all at once, and stir until blended. Turn dough onto a generously floured board and knead gently with tips of fingers, just enough to form into a ball. Pat the dough to a thickness of ½ an inch.

Cut into fingers, rounds or diamonds in the size you prefer. Roll both sides of the biscuits in the melted butter, then place them in any remaining melted butter in the pan and bake in a 450° oven 15-18 minutes, or until brown and done.

Top with cold berries and serve. Yield: 16-18 2-inch biscuits.

JAM OMELETTE

You'll find this one of the easiest dessert omelettes. I make mine at the table in an electric frying pan—everybody enjoys the proceedings, which seem to double the pleasure of eating the result.

1 tbsp. butter
1 tbsp. blanched almonds, slivered
6 eggs
1 tbsp. sugar
3 tbsp. cold water
1 tbsp. red currant jelly
2 tbsp. raspberry jam or jelly

Melt the butter in the omelette pan and brown the slivered almonds. Beat the eggs lightly with the sugar and cold water. Pour over the almonds and cook according to directions. When ready, place the red currant jelly and raspberry jam or jelly in the middle and fold the omelette. Serves 4-5.

TREACLE TART

This Norfolk specialty is true to the original recipe when made with golden syrup and English black treacle. This version has no bread crumbs, and it freezes very well.

pie dough of your choice
1 cup golden syrup
2 tbsp. treacle
2 tbsp. butter
grated rind of ½ a lemon
2 eggs, well beaten with
3 tbsp. cream

Line an 8-inch pie plate with pie dough, bake and let cool. Warm syrup, then add treacle. Remove from heat, add butter, lemon rind, and stir until butter is melted. Thoroughly stir in the eggs beaten with cream.

Pour into cooled crust and cook in a 350° oven until custard is set, about 15-20 minutes. Let cool, then top with whipped cream or chopped walnuts. Serves 4-6.

Note: The golden syrup and treacle can be replaced by 1¼ cups of molasses for a slightly different flavor.

GOLDEN SNOW FLUFF

Cool and light, this dessert is superb served with fresh strawberries, sweetened with Cointreau, Grand Marnier or sugar. The sauce is served separately.

2 envelopes unflavored gelatine
½ cup boiling water
1 cup sugar
½ tsp. salt
1 cup fresh grapefruit juice
1 cup fresh orange juice
4 eggs, separated
2 cups light cream or milk
⅓ cup sugar
pinch of salt
grated peel of 1 orange

Soak the gelatine in ½ cup of cold water 5 minutes. Add boiling water and stir until gelatine is dissolved. Add sugar, salt, and stir again to dissolve sugar (over low heat, if necessary). Add 2 juices, mix and refrigerate until the consistency is that of unbeaten egg whites. Then beat until fluffy with a rotary beater.

Beat egg whites until stiff and fold into fruit fluff. Pour into a glass dish, cover and refrigerate until set.

Orange Custard Sauce: Beat egg yolks with cream or milk, sugar and salt. Cook in top of a double boiler over medium-high heat to a light custard consistency, stirring often. Add orange peel, pour into a jug and refrigerate. Serves 10.

ORANGE AND LEMON SNOW

Snows are used mostly for desserts. Basically they are a sweet, light, fluffy aspic—very nice as a garnish to fruit salads. Vary the fruit juice; frozen undiluted concentrate can be used. It usually comes in 6-oz. cans, so water, apple juice or fresh orange juice can replace the balance of the liquid.

1 envelope unflavored gelatin
½ cup sugar
¼ tsp. salt
1½ cups fresh orange juice
¼ cup fresh lemon juice
2 unbeaten egg whites
peel of 1 orange and 1 lemon, grated

Mix the gelatin thoroughly with the sugar and salt in a small saucepan. Add ½ cup of the orange juice. Place over low heat, stirring constantly until the gelatin is dissolved.

Remove from heat and stir in the remaining orange juice and the lemon juice. Chill until slightly thicker than unbeaten egg white consistency.

When ready, add the unbeaten egg whites and the grated peel of orange and lemon, and beat with an electric beater until mixture foams up and begins to hold its shape. Spoon into glass dessert dish, or into small molds, and chill until firm.

To serve as a dessert, top with thawed frozen berries of your choice, or a custard sauce made with the remaining 2 egg yolks. Serves 8.

CARAMELIZED FLOATING ISLAND

A light, creamy, crunchy Victorian delight, this is one of those recipes that varies with every family. One variation is to replace the first ½ cup of sugar with maple sugar or syrup.

4 eggs, separated
1¼ cups sugar
2½ cups milk
vanilla or nutmeg, to taste

Beat the egg yolks with ½ a cup of the sugar until fluffy. Beat egg whites until soft peaks appear. Add ¼ cup of sugar and beat again until stiff.

Heat milk to a simmer in a large saucepan, then drop in egg white by heaping tablespoonfuls. When well puffed, turn quickly to cook other side. As soon as done, remove with a skimmer to a hot platter. These egg white balls take but a minute to cook.

Add yolks to milk and stir quickly until you have a lovely golden cream (don't allow it to boil). Flavor to taste and pour over egg whites.

Over medium heat, caramelize remaining sugar with 3 tbsp. of water to obtain a light golden syrup. Using a fork, pour caramel in long shreds over egg snow and let cool. Serves 6.

MAPLE TOURLOUCHE

This is a sort of quick upside-down cake and a must in the sugaring season in Eastern Canada. It should be served hot with cold rich cream poured on top. As a variation, add some chopped walnuts to the hot syrup.

1 cup maple syrup
1 tbsp. soft butter
3 tbsp. sugar
1 egg
1 cup all-purpose flour
2 tsp. baking powder
⅛ tsp. salt
¼ tsp. nutmeg or cinnamon
½ cup milk

Bring syrup to a boil and pour into a generously buttered 8 x 8 x 2-inch baking dish. Let stand in a warm place. With a large spoon or blending fork, beat butter, sugar and egg together until creamy.

Mix remaining dry ingredients and add with the milk to creamed mixture, stirring until well blended. Place as four large balls into hot syrup, then stretch dough with two forks until all are joined together. This is easy because the dough gets very soft when it comes in contact with the hot syrup.

Bake at 350° for 30 minutes, or until golden brown. When done, invert on a platter or serve directly from pan.

SUGAR PIE

Every summer, requests pour in for this sugary, yet creamy pie from people who have travelled in Quebec and had it in restaurants, and are looking for the recipe—which is almost as old as Canada. The following is made the way grand-mère taught me, though there are all kinds of recipes.

pastry of your choice
½ tsp. soda
¼ tsp. vanilla
1½ cups maple syrup
1 cup all-purpose flour
1 cup dark brown sugar
pinch nutmeg
⅓ cup butter

Line a 9-inch pie plate with pastry. Stir soda and vanilla into syrup and pour into pastry. Blend remaining ingredients with your fingertips until mixture is crumbly, then spread over syrup. Place a piece of foil under pan, because the pie often bubbles over. Bake at 350° for 30 minutes and let cool—it is best cold.

GRANITA DI CAFFE

This refreshing Florentine specialty is one of the most simple frozen desserts to prepare. Nothing can beat the pleasant refreshing sensation of the Granita on a hot afternoon. Black roasted coffee is used in the original recipe, but I have found that instant coffee gives a deeper flavor.

4 tbsp. instant coffee
2 cups boiling water
¼-½ cup sugar
2 tsp. vanilla *or*
1 tsp. aromatic orange bitters (Angostura)
whipped cream (optional)

Combine the instant coffee, boiling water and ¼-½ cup sugar (according to taste) in a saucepan and stir over medium heat just until the sugar is dissolved. Do not boil the mixture. Cool, and add the vanilla or bitters. Pour mixture into a shallow pan or a refrigerator freezing tray and freeze until almost firm. Turn into a bowl and beat well—an electric hand beater is ideal because it will beat more air into the mixture and make it lighter. Freeze until it is the consistency of sherbet.

To serve, spoon into sherbet glasses or punch cups and top with unsweetened, whipped cream to taste. Serves 4.

CONTINENTAL ICE CREAM

This is a great dessert to serve when raspberries are in season. Although it is quickly prepared, it is an elegant and refined dessert.

1 pint fresh raspberries
¼-½ cup red currant jelly
2 tbsp. brandy or port (optional)
6 dry almond macaroons
¼ cup slivered almonds
1 pint raspberry or strawberry ice cream

Clean the raspberries. Melt the currant jelly over low heat and pour over the berries. Stir gently with a rubber spatula until all the berries are covered with the jelly. Add the brandy or port and refrigerate until ready to serve.

Crumble the macaroons coarsely and mix in the almonds. To serve, put the ice cream in sherbet glasses and top with a generous portion of the raspberry sauce. Sprinkle the macaroon-almond mixture over. Serves 6.

FRESH APRICOT DRESSING FOR FRUIT SALAD

I like this so much that every season I freeze some mashed fresh apricots with sugar and lime juice. In the winter, I thaw the mixture and add the rest of the ingredients to make the dressing.

6-8 very ripe apricots (about 1 cup mashed)
juice of 1 fresh lime
3 tbsp. sugar
2 tbsp. mayonnaise
1 cup heavy cream, whipped
few drops of yellow coloring

Halve the apricots and remove pits. Blend in a blender for 3 seconds, or force through a sieve to make a purée. Add the lime juice and sugar; stir until well blended. (If you want to freeze the mixture, do it at this point.)

Add the mayonnaise and fold this mixture into the whipped cream. Color to taste.

Pile on fruit salad. For a sophisticated garnish, top with a few green pistachio nuts. Yield: 2½ cups.

BUTTER CRUMB GINGERBREAD

This is a delicious, crunchy, butter-topped gingerbread with a golden color and it keeps very well. I found this recipe in a 1935 English magazine, and to this day I have baked it with the same excellent results.

2 cups cake flour *or*
1⅔ cups all-purpose flour
1 tsp. baking soda
1 cup sugar
1 tsp. cinnamon
2 tsp. ginger
¼ tsp. salt
½ cup shortening or soft chicken fat
2 tbsp. molasses
1 egg
1 cup buttermilk

Topping:

2 tbsp. butter, very soft
1 tbsp. flour
4 tbsp. sugar
½ tsp. cinnamon or ginger

Sift together, three times, the flour, soda, sugar, cinnamon, ginger and salt. Cut in the shortening or chicken fat until a fine crumb mixture is obtained. Beat the molasses and egg together well and add to the crumb mixture. Add the buttermilk, mix well and pour into a greased 8 x 8 x 2-inch pan.

For the topping, spread the very soft butter lightly over the top. Mix together the flour, sugar, cinnamon or ginger and sprinkle on top of the buttered batter. Bake at 350° for 45 minutes.

OLD-FASHIONED HOT GINGERBREAD

This may be baked early and warmed up at 300°. Our grandmothers used to call it soft gingerbread—the cookie was the snap or hard gingerbread—and it is delicious served with beaten butter and green applesauce or stewed rhubarb.

½ cup sugar
½ cup molasses *or*
English treacle
¼ cup melted butter *or*
bacon fat
2¼ cups all-purpose flour
1 cup hot water minus 2 tbsp. (⅞ cup)
½-1 tsp. ginger
1 tsp. baking soda

Mix the sugar, molasses or treacle and melted butter or bacon fat. Add the flour and stir until thoroughly mixed.

Mix the hot water, ginger and baking soda and add all at once to the flour mixture. Mix enough to blend everything together.

Pour the batter into a well-buttered 8 x 8 x 2-inch pan. (If you use a Pyrex or pyroceram dish, it won't have to be unmolded.) Bake at 350° for 30-35 minutes, or until well done.

SUPERB PLUM PUDDING

Another gift from the British settlers.

½ cup grated unpeeled apples
¼ lb. chopped beef suet
¼ cup chopped walnuts
2 tbsp. diced candied orange peel
2 tbsp. diced candied lemon peel
⅔ cup diced candied citron peel
1½ cups seedless raisins
1 cup currants
1 tbsp. cinnamon
1½ tsp. ginger
¼ tsp. nutmeg
½ tsp. allspice
¼ tsp. salt
1 cup sugar
⅓ cup apricot jam
2 cups fine dry breadcrumbs

4 eggs
2 tbsp. milk
⅓ cup brandy or rum
⅓ cup white wine or orange juice

In a large bowl, combine all the ingredients except the last 4 and mix thoroughly. Beat the eggs, then add to them the remaining ingredients. Add to the fruit mixture and mix thoroughly with your hands—a spoon cannot blend this thick mass properly.

Oil and sugar a 1-quart mold or two 1-pint molds. Fill ⅔ full, cover tightly and steam—the quart for 5½ hours, the pints for 4. Serve with Special Hard Sauce.

Special Hard Sauce

½ cup unsalted butter
1½ cups sifted icing sugar (measure after sifting)
1 egg yolk
2 tbsp. rum or brandy

Cream the butter until very light. Gradually add the sifted icing sugar. When it is very smooth, add the egg yolk and the rum or brandy. Beat well, pour into a dish and refrigerate overnight.

APPLE MINCEMEAT

Make ahead of time for Christmas—refrigerated, it will keep 4 months; frozen will keep 1 year.

2 apples
1 lb. currants
1 lb. seedless raisins
¾ lb. fresh, ground beef suet
1 lb. brown sugar
¾ lb. mixed peel
3 tbsp. cinnamon
2 tbsp. allspice
1 tbsp. ground coriander
1½ cups dry sherry
4 tbsp. brandy

Peel, core and chop apples finely. Place in a bowl with the remaining ingredients and stir for 5 minutes. Pour into hot sterilized jars. Seal when cold. Yield: 3 pints.

CARAMEL APPLE CRUMBLE

An unusual apple crisp type of dessert.

4 large apples
1 cup light brown sugar
½ tsp. cinnamon
2 tbsp. rum
1 cup all-purpose flour
½ tsp. salt
1 cup grated medium cheddar cheese
½ cup soft butter

Peel, core and slice the apples thinly into an 8-inch baking dish. Mix ½ cup of the brown sugar with the cinnamon and rum. Sprinkle on the apples and mix lightly.

Combine flour, salt, grated cheese, butter and remaining ½ cup brown sugar.

Crumble mixture evenly over the apples. Bake in a 325° oven, 40 to 45 minutes. Serve warm with sour cream or whipped cream. Serves 4.

SHAKER BOILED APPLES

I wonder if the simplicity of this dessert explains its delicate flavor. Serve quite cold.

6 red cooking apples, unpeeled and uncored
cold water or apple juice
½ cup sugar

Place apples in a large saucepan. Add enough water to measure a half inch deep. Pour sugar over apples. Boil gently about 20 minutes or until apples are tender. Turn apples carefully several times. Serve with the sugar syrup. Serves 6.

APPLE PANCAKES

A luncheon dessert or a breakfast treat. Serve with a bowl of cinnamon sugar: a teaspoon of cinnamon mixed with a cup of sugar.

**1⅞ cups milk
2 eggs, beaten
2 cups flour
4 tsp. baking powder
2 tbsp. sugar
1 tsp. salt
2 tbsp. melted butter
4 medium apples, peeled, cored and grated
juice and grated rind of 1 lemon**

Add beaten eggs to milk, whip a few seconds. Sift together the flour, baking powder, sugar and salt. Add to milk mixture, stir only enough to moisten dry ingredients. Stir in the melted butter, again do not beat as texture toughens if beaten. Stir together the grated apple, lemon juice and rind. Add to pancake batter.

Bake on greased hot griddle or frying pan over medium high heat, turning only once, when bubbles appear on top. Bake and serve. Yield: 15 to 20 medium pancakes.

CROQUANTS AUX POMMES

An old recipe from Québec. Almost like a bonbon. Serve as is or with ice cream.

Peel, core and slice 2 large apples. Place in a bowl with ½ cup chopped nuts. Beat 1 egg with 1 cup sugar until well beaten to partly dissolve the sugar. Add 2 tablespoons flour and 1 teaspoon baking powder, ⅛ teaspoon salt. Pour into a 9-inch pie plate. Bake 35 minutes in a 375° oven, or until top is browned. Chill 6 to 8 hours before serving. Serves 4.

BEVERAGES

KIR

Abbé Kir of France is credited with the creation of this simply made but sophisticated drink.

⅓ cup Crème de Cassis* *or*
Cherry Heering liqueur
26-oz. bottle Chablis *or*
other good dry white wine, chilled

Chill six 6-oz. wine glasses. Pour 1 tbsp. of the Crème de Cassis into each, top with chilled wine and stir. Serves 6.

*Use the black currant liqueur, or non-alcoholic syrup.

DUTCH MILK PUNCH

Make this in a blender in front of your guests and serve it in chilled punch cups or wine glasses filled with crushed ice.

1 cup brandy
2 cups cold milk
4 tbsp. fine sugar
½ tsp. vanilla
fresh nutmeg, to taste

Pour the brandy into blender with milk, sugar and vanilla. Cover and blend at high speed until mixture is frothy. Pour over ice and grate a dash of nutmeg on top. Serves 6.

CALIFORNIA COLD DUCK

I was surprised when I saw "Cold Duck" on a breakfast menu, and was ready to pass it by. Now I'm glad I didn't; this version is a perfect before-dinner drink for a summer's night.

6 cubes sugar
2 cups fresh orange juice
26-oz. bottle extra dry domestic champagne, chilled

Use 6 champagne glasses, 5- or 6-oz. capacity, for this. Place 1 cube of sugar in each, divide fresh orange juice equally among glasses and top with well-chilled champagne. Serves 6.

RASPBERRY PUNCH

In the summer I use fresh berries—2 large cupfuls crushed with the sugar and strained to remove the seeds.

1 box frozen raspberries
¼ cup sugar
grated rind of 1 orange
¼ to ½ cup brandy
1 bottle red wine
(Canadian Bordeaux type or imported rosé)
1 bottle sparkling red wine *or*
1 large bottle soda

Place the frozen raspberries in a bowl, add the sugar to taste and grated orange rind. Let stand until the berries have thawed and the sugar has melted. Add brandy. (If desired the mixture may be strained to get rid of the raspberry seeds.) Mix well and add the red wine. This mixture may be kept in bottles, refrigerated, for 3 to 5 weeks.

To serve punch—pour mixture into a bowl and add the sparkling wine or soda. Serves 8.

MY ZIPPY FRESH BLENDER COCKTAIL

Here a blender is needed and there can be no substitute. This is one of the most interesting ways to use celery leaves.

2 well-packed cups celery leaves
2 thinly sliced unpeeled lemons
4-6 tbsp. honey *or* maple syrup

1 cup uncooked long grain
2 carrots, peeled and grated
¼ cup green onions, chopped
¼ cup parsley, minced
¼ cup celery and leaves, finely chopped
1 cup cooked green peas

Dressing:

½ tsp. salt
¼ tsp. pepper
¼ tsp. dry mustard
1 pinch sugar
2 tbsp. cider or wine vinegar
4 tbsp. salad oil

Cook rice according to directions on package. Cool, and place in a bowl.

To the cooled rice add the carrots, green onions, parsley, celery leaves and green peas.

Blend together the salt, pepper, dry mustard, sugar, cider or wine vinegar and salad oil. Pour over the rice, stir lightly with a fork until well mixed. Garnish with quartered hard-cooked eggs and a few tomato slices.

MISCELLANEOUS ACCOMPANIMENTS

ROMANIAN PICKUP

A recipe to prepare the night before so you'll have a healthy, invigorating start to a busy day.

1 sweet apple
juice of ½ a lemon
10-oz. carton plain yogurt
clear honey, to taste

Wash and core apple, then slice it thinly or grate on a medium grater. Immediately mix with the lemon juice. Thoroughly stir in yogurt and dribble honey on top. Cover and refrigerate overnight. Serves 1.

TOMATO-LEMON JAM

An old-fashioned preserve that never loses its appeal, my grandmother used either red or yellow tomatoes for this.

5 lbs. firm tomatoes, peeled
5 lbs. sugar
3 unpeeled lemons, thinly sliced
1 tbsp. grated fresh ginger root *or*
1 tsp. ground ginger

Chop peeled tomatoes coarsely and place in a saucepan in alternate layers with sugar and lemon slices. Add ginger (fresh, if possible) and stirring frequently, simmer slowly over medium-low heat until thick, about 45 to 50 minutes (it must have the consistency of jam). Pour into hot sterilized glasses and seal immediately. Yield: 4-5 glasses, 6 oz. each.

CRANBERRY TANGERINE RELISH CUPS

A festive turkey should be accompanied by a festive garnish. These would do any bird proud.

8 tangerines
8-oz. can whole cranberry sauce *or*
2 cups fresh sauce
⅛ tsp. mint extract

Cut about one-fourth off the stem end of each tangerine. Using a large spoon and working over a bowl, insert the tip of a spoon between the tangerine's meat and outer peel. Revolve the tangerine, working the spoon farther in each time and pulling the meat away —as it becomes loosened it's easy to insert the spoon all the way and gently scoop out the entire centre in one piece, leaving a perfect tangerine shell.

Do the same with each tangerine, setting the shells aside. Working over the same bowl, separate tangerine centres into sections, removing any seeds. Mix with juice, remaining ingredients, and chill. Spoon into shells and serve with turkey, chicken, duck, goose, pork or ham. Serves 8.

MY APPLESAUCE FOR MEAT

Serve hot with roast pork, ham, duck, goose or sausages.

2 lbs. apples, peeled, quartered and cored
2 tbsp. water
2 whole cloves
2 tbsp. sugar
3 tbsp. butter
juice and grated rind of ½ a lemon

Place in a saucepan the apples, water, cloves and sugar. Cover and simmer over low heat until apples are soft. Remove cloves. Add butter, lemon juice and rind and whisk until smooth. Serve hot. Yield: 1 pint.

CITRUS DRESSING FOR STUFFED ROAST PORK

This citrus dressing is the best I know of for pork. It can be used for a crown roast of pork, or for a boned leg of pork. To serve with a roast loin of pork, bake the dressing separately.

¼ cup butter
1 cup diced celery
1 large onion, diced
2 medium-size apples, peeled and chopped
6 cups diced bread
1 tsp. ground sage
¼ tsp. ground marjoram
1 can (8 oz.) whole cranberry sauce
¼ cup brown sugar
1 tsp. salt
grated rind of 1 orange
½ cup fresh orange juice

Melt the butter in a frying pan and add celery, onion and apples. Stir over medium-low heat until softened, but do not brown. Add diced bread, sage and marjoram. Place in a saucepan the cranberry sauce, brown sugar, salt and orange rind. Stir together over low heat until the sugar is dissolved. Add to the bread mixture. Add the orange juice gradually, continuing to mix until the bread is moistened. It is now ready to use as a stuffing for any type of roast pork.

To bake separately, put in a baking dish and bake, covered, at 350° for 1 hour.

FRESH ONION CUCUMBER RELISH

It takes but a minute and goes so well with a ham loaf, for instance.

2 sweet onions, thinly sliced
1 peeled cucumber, thinly sliced
3 tbsp. cider vinegar
⅓ cup peanut oil
1 tsp. salt
¼ cup minced parsley

Place all the ingredients in a screw-top jar. Cover and give it a few shakes. Let stand covered from 2 days to 3 weeks. Shake well before serving. This relish loses its crispness if not kept cool, but does not spoil or lose its flavor.

TOMATO CONCASSE

Despite its name, this sauce isn't French, but a specialty of Sweden. Use it on fresh trout or salmon, rice or an omelet.

6-8 tomatoes
1 small onion, finely chopped
2 tbsp. salad oil
1 crushed clove garlic
1 tbsp. finely chopped parsley
¼ tsp. each tarragon and fresh dill or dill seeds
½ tsp. sugar or honey

Pour boiling water over the tomatoes in a bowl, let stand 3 minutes, then peel and cut in half. Discard squeezed out juice and seeds, and chop tomatoes coarsely.

Fry onion in oil until golden brown here and there. Mix in well the tomatoes and remaining ingredients, cover and simmer over low heat 20-25 minutes (don't boil or overcook, it's the slow simmering that's important). Season to taste. Serves 4.

TARTAR SAUCE

This sauce is the classic accompaniment to fried and baked fish, but it's also good with things like fried mushrooms.

1 cup mayonnaise
2 tbsp. finely chopped sour pickles
1 tbsp. capers
1 small onion, finely chopped
3 sprigs parsley, chopped

Mix ingredients and chill at least 3 hours. Very nice served in a cup of crisp lettuce leaves. Yield: 1 cup.

GRAND-MERE'S COOKED DRESSING

Covered and refrigerated, this will keep 4-8 weeks in a glass jar. It is fine with all types of vegetable salads.

3 tbsp. butter
2 tbsp. all-purpose flour
1½ tsp. salt
1 tsp. dry mustard
1 tbsp. sugar
sprinkling of mace or nutmeg
1¼ cups milk or cream
2 egg yolks
⅓ cup cider vinegar
½ onion, peeled and sliced

Melt the butter in a heavy metal saucepan. Mix in the flour, salt, mustard, sugar and mace or nutmeg. Blend completely into the butter and add 1 cup of the milk. Cook over low heat, stirring most of the time, until mixture is slightly thickened and creamy.

Beat the remaining ¼ cup of milk together with the egg yolks. Stir into the hot mixture, beating well as they are added. When well mixed, add the remaining ingredients (be sure to use cider vinegar only). Simmer over low heat until thickened. Cool, remove the onion slices and refrigerate. Makes 1½ cups.

LEMON DRESSING

This is an excellent basic dressing for a green salad. A teaspoon of chopped fresh herbs, when available, can make interesting variations; basil, tarragon, chives, parsley, coriander, marjoram or thyme are the best. They must be fresh as must the lemon juice.

⅔ cup salad oil
½ cup fresh lemon juice
¼ tsp. each sugar and dry mustard
¼ tsp. freshly ground black pepper
1 whole garlic clove
1 tsp. salt

Place all the ingredients in a screw-top jar and shake vigorously until blended. Remove garlic after a few days; the dressing will keep about a month in a cool place (preferably not the refrigerator). Yield: 1 cup.

BLENDER MUSTARD HOLLANDAISE

Use your blender for a minute and you'll have perfect hollandaise. If you don't have a blender, follow your favorite recipe and add the teaspoon of mustard when the sauce is cooked.

4 egg yolks
2 tbsp. fresh lemon juice
1 cup (½ lb.) butter
4 tsp. very hot water
½ tsp. salt
few drops of Tabasco
1 tsp. Dijon-style mustard

Combine the egg yolks and lemon juice in blender, cover and blend 10 seconds at high speed. Melt butter until it bubbles. Gradually add hot water to yolks while blending at medium speed, then add hot butter in a slow, steady stream.

Turn off blender, add remaining ingredients, cover and blend at high speed 30 seconds. Pour into a serving dish, cover and keep at room temperature. It's best to make this early on the day it's needed rather than the day before. Yield: 2 cups.

MAPLE SYRUP BAKED BEANS

This is one of my family's recipes. I have never seen the apple cove in any cookbook, and have no idea where my mother got the idea—maybe it was her own. These are very, very good beans.

4 cups dried navy beans
12 cups cold water
1 tsp. soda
1 lb. fat and lean salt pork, sliced

1 large onion
1 tsp. dry mustard
1 cup maple syrup
1 tbsp. coarse salt
4 cored apples, unpeeled
1 cup maple or light brown sugar
½ cup butter
½ cup rum (optional)

Preheat oven to 325°.

Cover the beans with 12 cups cold water. Let soak overnight. In the morning, pour the whole thing in a large saucepan. Add 1 teaspoon soda and more cold water to cover the beans, if necessary. Bring to a boil, uncovered, then boil until some of the skins come off when you blow on the beans.

Line a bean pot with the sliced pork, then pour in the beans and their water. Roll the onion in the dry mustard until all of the mustard sticks to it, then bury it in the middle of the beans. Pour the maple syrup and coarse salt on top.

Bake 4-5 hours in a 325° oven. In the last hour of cooking, cover the beans with the whole apples, placed as closely together as possible. Cream the sugar and butter together, then spread the mixture on top of the apples. This forms a most delicious topping when the beans are baked. Pour the rum on top just before serving. Serves 8-10.

BUCKWHEAT KASHA CASSEROLE

If you like the flavor of buckwheat, you will find this casserole one of the best. Nice for lunch with a green salad.

1 box medium buckwheat Kasha
2 to 3 tbsp. butter
salt, pepper to taste
1 to 2 cups cottage cheese
2 eggs
3 to 4 green onions, chopped (optional)

Cook the box of buckwheat kasha according to directions on the box. When done, add the butter, salt and pepper.

Place half in a deep casserole. Mix together the cottage cheese, eggs and green onions. Place over the kasha. Top with the rest of the kasha.

Bake, uncovered, in a 350° oven for 20 to 25 minutes. Serves 6.

APPLE CHEESE BREAD

Apple and sharp cheddar combine to give a tangy and sweet flavor to this quick bread. I always keep some frozen for emergencies. Thirty minutes in a 325° oven will thaw it, ready to be served for tea or breakfast with butter and marmalade.

½ cup shortening
⅔ cup sugar
2 eggs, beaten
1½ cups grated unpeeled apples
½ cup grated sharp cheddar cheese
¼ cup chopped walnuts
2 cups all-purpose flour
1½ tsp. baking powder
½ tsp. each soda and salt

Cream shortening and sugar, add eggs and mix well. Add apples and nuts, blend the whole together. Add sifted dry ingredients and mix lightly. Bake in a well-greased 9 x 5-inch loaf pan in a 350° oven 50 to 60 minutes.

COTTAGE CHEESE BISCUITS

Lightly textured inside, crispy and crusty on top, these biscuits can be served for breakfast, with fruit and salad or soup—or with the main course instead of bread.

1 egg, lightly beaten
3 tbsp. milk
1 cup cottage cheese, any kind
2 tbsp. butter, melted
2 scant cups all-purpose flour
4 tsp. baking powder
1 tsp. salt
¼ cup fresh parsley, minced

Preheat the oven to 450°. Mix the egg, milk, cottage cheese and butter thoroughly.

Stir together the flour, baking powder, salt and parsley. Add to the first mixture and blend with the fingertips. If necessary, add more milk, a few drops at a time, to make the dough hold together.

Turn on to a floured board and knead for 30 seconds. Pat into a shape ½-inch thick, then cut into 18 squares.

Place on a greased baking sheet and bake for about 12 minutes or until golden brown.

COMPLETE MENUS

BEEF FILLET DINNER

A simple but elegant dinner for 6.

Milli Fanti Consommé
Beef Fillet Connaught
Swedish Glazed Potatoes
Poblano Beets
Ruby Apple Sauce

Milli Fanti Consommé

¾ cup fresh fine breadcrumbs
½ cup grated Parmesan cheese
2 whole eggs, beaten
salt and pepper, to taste
⅛ tsp. grated nutmeg
6 cups hot chicken or beef consommé

Blend together the breadcrumbs, Parmesan cheese and eggs. Add salt, pepper and nutmeg. Pour into the hot consommé. Cover and simmer over low heat, 8 minutes. Beat with a whisk.

Beef Fillet Connaught

1 3- to 3½-lb. beef fillet
3 tbsp. butter
1 tbsp. salad oil
3 to 4 onions, thinly sliced
1 tsp. strong prepared mustard
1 tbsp. chutney
¼ cup Madeira wine

Trim and tie the fillet. Heat the butter and oil in a large frying pan. Brown fillet on both sides, over high heat, turning all the time. Set aside in dripping pan. Add onions to remaining fat in the pan. Brown over medium heat.

Meanwhile blend the mustard and chutney. Salt and pepper the fillet. Spread chutney mixture on top. Pile onion over. Pour Madeira around.

Roast in preheated 400° oven exactly 30 minutes, for rare, 40 for medium well done. Make gravy with canned beef consommé undiluted added to pan drippings.

Swedish Glazed Potatoes

Boil 6 to 8 medium-size potatoes, with peel. Do not overcook. Drain. Cool. Peel and set aside, covered. This can be done 6 to 8 hours prior to dinner. Keep covered, at room temperature. When meat gravy is ready, pour ¼ cup in frying pan, add 1 teaspoon butter and ½ teaspoon thyme. Add potatoes, stir, uncovered, over medium heat, until golden and hot. Serves 6.

Poblano Beets

4 beets
¼ cup grapefruit or orange juice
½ tsp. sugar
1 tbsp. butter
1 tbsp. lemon juice
1 cup seedless grapes

Peel and grate the raw beets, cook with the grapefruit and orange juice, sugar, butter and lemon juice. Cover and cook for 1 hour, stirring occasionally. Twenty minutes before the end of the cooking period, add the grapes. The fruit juice may be replaced by grape juice or red wine.

Ruby Applesauce

4 to 5 cups blue Concord grapes
6 apples
½ to 1 cup sugar
1 lemon
whipped cream (optional)
grated unsweetened chocolate

Wash the grapes. Pinch the skins from the pulp; reserve the skins.
Put the pulp in a saucepan, bring to a boil, and simmer for about 5 minutes. Put through a strainer to remove the seeds.

Peel the apples, core and slice thin. Put the apples, grape pulp and skins, sugar to taste, and the juice and grated rind of the lemon in a saucepan. Bring to a boil, while stirring.

Simmer over medium heat for 8 to 12 minutes, until the sauce has a nice texture. Taste for sweetness and add more sugar if necessary, but remember the sauce will be sweeter when it is cold.

Serve well chilled, with or without whipped cream and grated chocolate.

This sauce can be frozen. It will keep frozen for 12 months. It takes 3 hours to defrost at room temperature. Serves 8 or more.

SALMON DINNER

A wonderful dinner for 6.

Sea Island Broiled Grapefruit
Victoria Salmon
Molded Fresh Mint Relish
Wild Rice Chasseur
Chinese Broccoli
Swedish Cream

Sea Island Broiled Grapefruit

3 grapefruits, cut in halves
¼ cup honey
4 tbsp. rum
½ tsp. ground cardamon
½ tsp. butter, for each half grapefruit

Mix together the honey, rum, ground cardamon. Spread on grapefruits. Top with butter. When they are prepared ahead of time, wrap in foil paper.

To serve, place on broiler, unwrapped, 3 to 4 inches away from heat. Broil 4 to 6 minutes.

Victoria Salmon

2 lbs. fresh salmon fillet
salt, pepper, paprika
lemon juice
flour
unsalted butter

Cut salmon fillet on an angle to make slices about ⅜ of an inch thick. Marinate in fresh lemon juice for 20 minutes. Dip in flour which has been seasoned with salt, pepper and paprika and fry in melted unsalted butter for about 20 or 30 seconds on each side. Drain on a paper towel. Garnish with parsley and lemon and serve immediately.

Molded Fresh Mint Relish

1½ envelopes unflavored gelatine
2 tbsp. water
1 cup hot water
8 whole cloves
10 aniseeds
¼ tsp. salt
¼ cup sugar
½ cup brandy
½ cup grapefruit juice
¼ cup each fresh lime and lemon juice
¼ cup chutney
¼ cup minced fresh mint

Add the gelatine to the cold water. Let stand 5 minutes.

Place in a saucepan the hot water, cloves, aniseeds, salt, sugar. Boil 5 minutes. Add brandy and grapefruit juices. Stir in the lime and lemon juice and the gelatine. Refrigerate until half set.

Stir in the chutney and minced fresh mint. Oil 6 individual molds. Fill. Refrigerate until set.

Wild Rice Chasseur

¾ to 1 cup wild rice*
2 tbsp. brandy
1 tbsp. curry
3 to 5 tbsp. chutney
¼ cup butter
salt and pepper to taste

Wash the rice several times in cold water. Bring to a boil 4 cups water. Add 1 teaspoon salt and 1 cup rice. Cover and simmer for 20 to 30 minutes. Simmered wild rice does not lose its nutty flavor.

109

Mix together the brandy and curry in a cup. Add the chutney.

Add to the rice, salt and pepper to taste, the butter, and stir with a fork until melted and serve.

You may replace the wild rice with a mixture of "Long Grain and Wild Rice" which is sold in packages.

Chinese Broccoli

1 lb. broccoli
3 tbsp. salad oil
1 small onion, diced
2 tbsp. soya sauce
1 tsp. sugar
1 pinch monosodium glutamate
½ cup chicken stock
1 tsp. cornstarch

Wash the broccoli and cut into 1-inch pieces. Heat the salad oil in a heavy frying pan and brown the onion. Then add the broccoli and cook over medium heat, stirring constantly for 3 minutes. Add soya sauce and sugar. Blend together the cornstarch and chicken stock. Add to the broccoli. Keep stirring over high heat for 1 minute.

Swedish Cream

2 envelopes unflavored gelatine
¼ cup cold water
1 pint heavy cream
1 cup sugar
2 cups commercial sour cream
1 tsp. vanilla extract
1 tsp. rosewater (optional)

Sprinkle gelatine over water. Let stand 5 minutes.

Heat heavy cream but do not boil it. Add the gelatine and sugar and stir until completely dissolved. Cool to room temperature.

Fold sour cream, vanilla extract and rosewater (optional) into the gelatine mixture. Pour into a dish and chill until set.

Serve plain, or top with sugared fresh fruits, frozen fruits, or jam.

SPRING DINNER FOR EIGHT HAPPY PEOPLE

The arrival of spring calls for rejoicing, and a good way of celebrating it is to delight your friends with a handsome dinner. This one serves 8 and most of it can be prepared in advance — even, except for the peas, cooked and frozen until needed.

The ultimate dinner blends a well-planned menu, perfect food and a beautiful table setting into a momentous whole, one that reflects the gay, light, airy mood of the season.

Cream of Curry Soup
Golden Cheese Crisps
Chicken Pie Terrapin
Green Peas Robert
Divine Strawberry Torte

Cream of Curry Soup

Serve this with the Cheese Crisps, or with garnishes of chopped green onion, grated unpeeled apple tossed with lemon juice, crumbled crisped bacon and chopped hard-boiled eggs. Pass a tray holding a small bowl of each and let your guests choose their favorite.

1 onion, finely chopped
2 tsp. curry powder
⅓ cup butter
⅔ cup flour
3 cups chicken bouillon
3 cups light cream
salt and pepper to taste
¼ cup dry sherry (optional)

Simmer onion with curry powder and butter, stirring most of time, until onion is soft but not browned. Add flour, mix thoroughly, then add bouillon and cream. Stir or, preferably, beat with a wire whisk until soup starts to boil. Simmer over low heat for 15 minutes.

If making the day before, stop here, let soup cool, then refrigerate. Reheat when needed.

Add salt, pepper and sherry.

111

Golden Cheese Crisps

They can be served with drinks if you are not using them with the soup. Prepare them in the morning, set on a baking sheet and heat when needed.

> **1 cup grated strong Cheddar cheese**
> **½ cup mayonnaise**
> **¼ tsp. Worcestershire sauce**
> **1 tsp. prepared mustard**
> **½ tsp. turmeric**
> **sesame seeds or finely chopped walnuts**
> **crackers, any type**

Blend cheese with mayonnaise, Worcestershire, mustard and turmeric. Spread on crackers and sprinkle with seeds or nuts. Bake at 400° for 5-8 minutes and serve warm. Yield: about 24 crisps.

Chicken Pie Terrapin

This chicken, with its special sauce and garnish of forcemeat balls, may seem like a lot of work, but the result is a beautiful and tasty pie that your guests will long remember.

> **2 chickens, 3 lbs. each**
> **¼ cup flour**
> **1 tsp. salt**
> **½ tsp. pepper**
> **½ tsp. tarragon or ¼ tsp. thyme**
> **3 tbsp. butter**
> **3 tbsp. salad oil**

Cut chickens into serving pieces. Roll them in mixture of flour and seasonings until well coated. Heat butter and oil in a large frying pan and brown 5 or 6 chicken pieces at a time until golden. When all are browned, put back into frying pan, cover and simmer over low heat 30 minutes.

In the meantime, make a stock with necks, gizzards, and bits of skin removed from chicken. Prepare forcemeat bread balls as follows:

8 slices crustless white bread
grated peel of 1 lemon
⅓ cup chopped parsley
¼ tsp. thyme
⅛ tsp. nutmeg
1 tsp. salt
¼ tsp. pepper
⅓ cup soft butter
2 egg yolks

Chop bread very fine or, if it's stale, grate on a coarse grater. Mix thoroughly in a bowl with lemon peel, parsley and seasonings. Add butter, egg yolks, and work into a smooth paste. Form into 1-inch balls by rolling with hands on a board. Set on a platter and refrigerate.

Then make savory forcemeat balls:

livers and hearts of 2 chickens
1½ cups twice-ground cooked ham
¼ cup chopped parsley
4 green onions, finely chopped
salt and pepper, to taste

Pass livers and hearts through a meat grinder and add to remaining ingredients. Blend, then form into 1-inch balls as previously. Brown both sets lightly in butter.

pastry of your choice
2 tbsp. cornstarch
½ cup cream, any type
1 beaten egg yolk or milk

To assemble pie, line a large casserole with pastry, put chicken in and place forcemeat balls among pieces. To juices remaining in frying pan, add 1 cup of strained chicken stock and boil fast, scraping bottom.

Mix cornstarch into cream, add to pan and stir over medium heat until creamy. Pour sauce over contents of casserole. Brush edge of crust with egg yolk or milk. Top casserole with pastry, pinch edges together and cut one slit in centre. Bake at 350° for 50-60 minutes, or until a deep golden color.

Green Peas Robert

A French chef, Robert, who's a master at cooking vegetables, uses frozen peas in this excellent recipe.

4 slices bacon, diced
1 small onion, chopped
2 tbsp. butter
2 pkgs. frozen green peas, 10 oz. each
¼ cup shredded lettuce leaves
½ tsp. sugar
salt and pepper, to taste

Fry bacon until crisp and drain on absorbent paper. Brown onion in bacon fat, remove, then drain fat from pan. Put butter in same pan and, when melted, add frozen peas, lettuce and sugar.

Cover tightly and simmer until peas are separated. Stir to mix, break up any stuck together, then cover again and cook until tender. Add bacon and onion, stir until hot, then season.

Divine Strawberry Torte

A wonderful party dessert, this cuts easily into wedges. The strawberries may be replaced with raspberries, peaches or blueberries, depending on the season, and everything can be done ahead of time.

½ cup egg whites
1 tbsp. lemon juice
pinch of salt
1⅓ cups fine granulated sugar
½ cup flaked coconut
2 egg yolks
pinch of salt
2 tbsp. lemon juice
2 tbsp. sugar
1 tbsp. cornstarch
½ cup water
1 cup whipping cream
1-2 pints fresh strawberries

Using hand mixer or electric beater, beat egg whites with lemon juice and salt until soft peaks are formed. Add sugar, 3 tbsp. at a time, beating hard at each addition. Keep beaten until a stiff meringue is formed, 10-15 minutes in all. Gently fold in coconut.

Mark a 9-inch circle on a baking sheet and grease inside lightly. Turn meringue into centre of circle and carefully spread to edges, building up until about 2 inches high around outside and slightly lower in centre. Enclose outer edge with a 2-inch foil collar.

Place in an oven that has been at 400° for 15 minutes. Immediately turn heat off and let meringue stand in closed oven 5 hours. Open door and leave in oven 5 hours or overnight.

To make lemon sauce: beat egg yolks with salt, lemon juice and sugar. Stir in cornstarch and water. Cook in a double boiler or over low heat until mixture thickens, beating often. Refrigerate covered until cold, then fold in cream whipped until stiff.

To serve, slip meringue shell on to a serving plate with a large spatula. Top with the lemon cream and arrange sweetened berries on top. Serve at once or refrigerate 2 hours.

GRAND DINER

A very special dinner for 16 guests.

This very elegant dinner has the quality of being almost completely prepared the day before. The last minute work does not have to be done by an expert. It is the kind of dinner that should have the proper setting, such as a lace cloth, silverware, your best glasses, candlelight and flowers.

Tapenade de Nice with Crudités
Melon Alcantara
Paupiettes of sole "à l'Ecossaise"
Vegetables Jardinière
Watercress Salad
Hot Brioches
Peaches Dijonaise
Filtered Coffee

Wines:

Iced Champagne served with Tapenade
Dry Sherry served with Melon
Chablis — Premier Cru served with Fish
French Liqueur served with Coffee

Tapenade de Nice

1 crust dry bread
1 clove garlic
3 tbsp. red wine vinegar
¼ lb. pine nuts (pignolia)
3 tbsp. capers
4 fillets of anchovy
2 hard-cooked eggs
12 black olives, pitted
¼ cup parsley, minced
1 cup olive oil
salt and pepper to taste
1 cucumber
1 green pepper
1 can artichoke hearts
2 carrots
6 hard-cooked eggs

Remove crust from a slice of bread, cut peeled garlic in two, rub both sides of the bread with the garlic. Break up the bread in a bowl, pour the vinegar on top. Work bread and vinegar with the fingers until it is mushy.

At this point, the work can be done either in a blender or by passing the ingredients through a food chopper. Place in the blender the bread, nuts, capers, fillets of anchovy, the yolks of the hard-cooked eggs (save whites for salad), black olives, parsley and the split clove of garlic. Add ½ cup of the olive oil. Blend until creamy. Gradually add the balance of the olive oil. When well blended, add salt and pepper to taste. The process is the same with the food mill, adding the oil gradually as the food is chopped.

Pour the mixture into a glass dish that can be fitted into an elegant bowl filled with ice. The tapenade can be prepared two or three days ahead of time. Keep refrigerated.

To serve, make small sticks of the cucumber, green pepper and carrots, cut the 6 hard-cooked eggs into quarters. Drain the artichoke hearts and spread on absorbent paper until thoroughly dry.

Place the prepared vegetables and eggs on the ice around the dish of tapenade sauce. Serve with a glass of cold champagne.

Melon Alcantara

Prepare individual servings in small ovenware dishes, refrigerate overnight if convenient. To serve, place in oven as indicated in the recipe.

2 cantaloups
1 Spanish melon
4 limes
salt
1 tbsp. fresh grated ginger
freshly grated nutmeg
¼ lb. butter

Make balls of cantaloup and melon, making a mixture of five to seven for each dish, depending on the dish. Salt and pepper and grate a dash of nutmeg over each one. Cut the butter into small dice and separate evenly over each one. Mix the freshly grated ginger and lime juice, divide evenly on top of the melon, cover and refrigerate.

To serve, place for 20 minutes in a 350° oven.

Paupiettes of Sole "à l'Ecossaise"

This dish can be prepared early morning to be served at night. Only the reheating in a 400° oven is left to be done before serving.

2 lbs. fresh salmon
2 eggs
½ cup minced parsley
1 tsp. tarragon, fresh or dried
1 tsp. salt
½ tsp. pepper
18 fillets of sole
grated rind of 3 lemons
1 bottle dry white wine
¼ cup butter
½ cup flour
1 cup rich cream
½ cup milk
3 tbsp. brandy
salt and pepper to taste
½ tsp. sugar

1 tbsp. butter
1 lb. fresh thinly sliced mushrooms *or*
1 large box of imported chanterelles
½ tsp. monosodium glutamate
1 green onion, chopped fine
salt and pepper

Pass the uncooked salmon, which has been filleted, through food chopper twice. Add the eggs, parsley, tarragon, salt and pepper and beat with a whip or a wooden spoon until creamy and blended.

Spread sole fillets on a table, salt and pepper each one lightly and sprinkle with a pinch of lemon rind. Butter the top with some of the salmon mixture, roll and tie with a thread.

In a large frying pan, warm up the white wine but do not let it boil. Place half the rolled fillets in the hot wine and simmer 10 minutes over low heat, basting constantly with the hot wine. Remove the fillets and place them next to each other on a service platter which can stand oven heat. Cook the balance in the same manner.

Pass the cooking wine through a fine strainer and set aside.

In the same frying pan, melt the ¼ cup butter, add flour, stir until very well blended, pour the strained wine over, add the cream and milk. Stir constantly with a wire whip, over medium heat, until you have a smooth, velvety sauce. Then add the brandy, sugar, salt and pepper to taste. Stir again for a few minutes. Taste for seasoning. If sauce is too thick, add a little milk or cream gradually, while stirring, until the consistency is right. Set aside.

Melt 1 tablespoon of butter, when light brown add the mushrooms, monosodium glutamate, chopped green onion, stir half a minute over high heat. Place here and there around the fish. Divide the sauce equally over each fillet of fish, leaving some of the mushrooms uncovered.

When ready to serve, place in a preheated 400° oven for 15 to 20 minutes.

Vegetables Jardinière
Make a selection of small green beans, small carrots and round balls of potatoes or any other mixture of vegetables suitable to you. Blanch according to rules, roll into creamed butter, mix and serve. Use 4 lbs. of vegetables for 16 people.

Watercress Salad

Mix together in a bowl watercress and Bibb lettuce, simply toss with a plain French dressing, garnish with the finely shredded remaining two egg whites from the Tapenade.

Peaches Dijonnaise

8 peaches
1 cup fresh orange juice
grated rind of two oranges
½ cup black currant syrup
1 cup sugar
1 cup water

Wash the peaches but do not peel. Place in a large frying pan with a cover, the orange juice and rind, the black currant syrup, sugar and water. Bring to a fast rolling boil, while stirring. Place the unpeeled peaches in the syrup, cover, lower the heat and simmer 25 minutes turning once. Remove from heat, uncover.

While the peaches are cooking, prepare the praline mixture.

Praline

2 cups sugar
juice of ½ a lemon
1 cup bleached almonds
1 cup unbleached hazelnuts

Place in a saucepan the sugar and lemon juice, stir constantly over medium heat until it has turned into a light golden syrup, add the nuts, stir until well mixed, pour mixture into a jelly roll pan, spreading the nuts and the syrup as well and as quickly as possible. Set aside until cold, which should take about one hour or so. Then either crush in a blender at high speed, a bit at a time, removing the blended part before adding more; or butter a rolling pin and crush a few pieces at a time over a wooden board. Set aside.

Peel the cooled peaches, cut in half. Place a half, rounded side up, in individual custard cups or soufflé dish, sprinkle 2 tablespoons of the praline over each and top with the following cream mixture.

119

French Cream

5 whole eggs
4 egg yolks
1 cup sugar
4 cups light cream
1 cup milk
1 vanilla bean

Beat together lightly the whole eggs, egg yolks and sugar. In the meantime, warm up the cream and milk with the vanilla bean. When hot, remove the vanilla bean, beat into egg and sugar mixture. Divide equally over the praline and peach.

Place the individual dishes in a pan of hot water, bake in a 350° oven until the blade of a knife comes out clean. When ready and cooled, refrigerate overnight or until ready to serve.

Serve with Dijon Syrup made in the following manner.

Dijon Syrup

1 cup sugar
1½ cups water
4 tbsp. vanilla
4 tbsp. coffee liqueur
1 tbsp. brandy

Place the sugar in a frying pan, stir over medium heat until it turns into a light golden syrup. Remove from heat. Add the cold water, a tablespoon at a time. When all is added, put back over the heat and cook, stirring occasionally, until the mixture has formed a light syrup. Remove from heat and cool. Then add the vanilla, coffee liqueur and brandy. Mix well. Place in a jar and refrigerate until ready to pour some over each dessert. This sauce can be kept refrigerated for 2 to 3 weeks.

ANY TIME OF THE YEAR BUFFET

Melon consommé (Spring and Summer) or
Piquant Pink Bouillon (Autumn and Winter)
Seafood Superb
Flemish Chicken Casserole
Rice Pilaff Orientale
Carrots Italienne
Braised Onions
Elegant and Casual Baba au Rhum
Café Noir

(All recipes will serve 6 — Double or triple as needed).

Melon Consommé:

Budget minded: top with minced chives or parsley.

For sheer elegance: top with caviar (Danish lumpfish gives the elegance without the cost). For a summer garden lunch: serve followed by cucumber sandwiches, cheese sticks and a basket of fruit.

2 cups melon balls
½ cup sherry
3 cans beef consommé
⅓ cup commercial sour cream
minced chives, parsley or caviar

Depending on the season choose the best melon or cantaloup available. Make the balls with a special little spoon called a baller, they can be very small or large. Place in dish that can be covered. Pour sherry on top and refrigerate overnight. Refrigerate also for the same period the unopened cans of consommé and the caviar.

To serve, open cans, place a few melon balls in the bottom of the cups, add a teaspoon of the sherry, cover by teaspoonfuls with half a can of the chilled, jellied consommé. Top each with a teaspoon of sour cream, a dot of minced chives or parsley or caviar on top of the cream. They can be prepared 25 to 40 minutes before serving and kept refrigerated.

Piquant Pink Bouillon

Serve boiling hot garnished with a half slice of lemon or float a crescent of peeled avocado on top. This delicious bouillon is a combination of ready-to-serve foods.

1 (8-ounce) can tomato sauce
1 (10½-ounce) can beef bouillon
2 can measures of cold water
1½ cups tomato juice
1 tsp. sugar
½ tsp. prepared horseradish
grated rind of ½ a lemon or 1 lime
⅛ tsp. tarragon or basil or thyme
¼ cup dry red wine

Combine in a saucepan all the ingredients except the wine. Simmer 15 minutes. Taste for salt and pepper. Add the wine. When hot, serve. This will give a 6-ounce portion for each serving.

Seafood Superb
A superb buffet salad, prepare all the ingredients a day or two ahead of time. Keep refrigerated in separate containers. An hour before serving, blend together and garnish. Vary the seafood according to the season. Fresh cooked salmon and crabmeat are very spring-like, use large shrimps in the winter, lobster in the fall.

12-18 medium-size shrimps, cooked and peeled
1 (7-ounce) can crabmeat
1 hard cooked egg, coarsely chopped
1 cup celery, finely chopped
4 red radishes, grated (in season)
1 medium carrot, grated
juice of 2 lemons
½ tsp. salt
⅛ tsp. mace
⅛ tsp. savory
1-1½ cups special dressing

Special dressing
1-1½ cups mayonnaise
1 tbsp. French mustard
1 tbsp. catsup
½ tsp. chili sauce
1 tbsp. each chopped pimiento and green pepper

minced chives and parsley to taste
1 hard cooked egg, chopped fine
1 tsp. prepared horseradish

To serve, place the shrimps in a mixing bowl, pick over the crabmeat to make sure all bones are removed and add to the shrimps, along with the egg, celery, radishes, carrot and lemon juice. Make the dressing by mixing the ingredients thoroughly, then add enough to the salad mixture to flavor well. Season with the salt, mace and savory. Blend gently but thoroughly. Set on a platter garnished with lettuce leaves, wedges of tomato and red radishes. Refrigerate until ready to serve. Can be prepared 1 hour before serving.

Flemish Chicken Casserole

The surprise is beer — the Flemish touch. Cook the day before the party, reheat, covered, in a 300° oven when ready to serve. This dish freezes well. Three Cornish hens, split in half, can replace the chicken.

3 to 3½-lb. chicken or
3 chicken breasts split in half
3 tbsp. butter
1 tsp. salt
1 large onion, diced
2 medium carrots, peeled and chopped
2 stalks celery, finely chopped
¼ tsp. marjoram
½ tsp. pepper
1 tsp. salt
1 tbsp. brown sugar
3 slices bacon
12 ounces light beer
juice of ½ a lemon
1 tsp. cornstarch
1 tbsp. water or brandy

Cut the chicken into small individual pieces or divide each chicken breast in two. Melt the butter in an ovenware casserole, an enamel cast iron type would have the Flemish touch. Add the onion, carrots, celery and marjoram, stir over low heat until the vegetables are well buttered. Add the salt, pepper, and brown sugar. Stir again to mix and add the chicken, stir to mix and top the whole with the slices of bacon. Cook, uncovered in a preheated 400° oven for 20 minutes. Then add the beer, cover and cook another 30 to 45 minutes or until the chicken is tender.

At this point, cool and refrigerate or freeze when made ahead of time.

To serve, heat until bubbly in a 300° oven. Blend together the lemon juice, cornstarch and cold water or brandy. Add to the sauce while stirring until slightly thickened. Taste for seasoning.

Rice Pilaff Orientale

An easy, easy way to cook rice — you can replace the currants or raisins by toasted almonds, lots of minced parsley, grated carrots, chopped green onions, a teaspoon of curry or turmeric blended with a tablespoon of brandy — each one will give an entirely different flavor to the rice.

3 tbsp. margarine

1 medium-size onion, chopped

2 cups long grain rice

4 cups cold water or chicken bouillon

1 tsp. salt

¼ cup currants

¼ cup boiling apple juice or white wine

Melt the margarine in a saucepan, add the onion, stir over high heat, until onion is buttery, add the rice and keep stirring until rice is toasted to a light brown color, lower heat if necessary. Then add, all at once, the 4 cups cold water or chicken bouillon and the salt. Let the whole boil hard over high heat, uncovered, until the water covering the rice is absorbed. This takes about 5 minutes.

In the meantime, pour the boiling apple juice or white wine over the currants. When the rice is ready, add the currants, stir, cover and cook 20 minutes over very low heat. The rest of the liquid will be absorbed by the rice, which will be beautifully cooked, each grain separated. Uncover, stir with a fork. Cover until ready to use, it will stay hot for 25 minutes.

To make the day before, cook, cool, refrigerate covered. To serve, pour ¼ cup water in saucepan, add the rice, cover and steam over very low heat for 15 minutes, stirring once. It is then hot and ready.

Carrots Italienne

These are equally good and exciting served hot or at room temperature or tepid. To vary, replace the Marsala wine by an equal quantity of Madeira or Port wine. For luncheon, use as a garnish for broiled liver and bacon. For dinner, serve with roast chicken or veal.

1½ lbs. (about 10 or 12) carrots
2 tbsp. butter or margarine
¼ tsp. sugar
½ cup Marsala wine
¼ cup water
minced parsley or chives
salt and pepper to taste

Peel and cut the carrots into long matchsticks. Melt the butter, when possible use a stainless steel saucepan. Add the carrots, stir gently until they are well coated with butter. Sprinkle with sugar. Add the Marsala and water. Bring to a boil. Cover, then simmer over very low heat for 20 minutes. Uncover and boil over high heat until liquid is reduced. Be careful not to let them burn. Salt and pepper to taste. Pour into serving dish. Sprinkle with parsley or chives. Serve hot or cover and let stand until ready to serve.

Braised Onions

For a party I use small white onions, about 1 to 2 inches in diameter—but all sizes are very tasty braised in the same manner. Only the cooking time will vary as larger onions have more juices, cook them until tender.

24 small white onions
½ cup chicken or beef consommé (canned type undiluted)
2 tbsp. butter
½ tsp. thyme
2 stalks parsley, left whole
½ a bay leaf
salt and pepper to taste

Peel the onions. Place in a heavy metal saucepan, just large enough to accommodate all the onions in a single row. I use a large frying pan. Pour the undiluted consommé on top of the onions, add the butter, thyme, parsley and bay leaf. Bring to a boil, then cover and simmer, about 25 to 30 minutes or until onions are tender, uncover, boil hard for 5 minutes. Salt and pepper to taste. Pour into serving dish. Serve hot or cooled to room temperature. When served hot, top with paprika; at room temperature, surround with watercress.

Elegant and Casual Baba au Rhum

With this recipe even a cake mix can fool many into thinking they are eating the real Baba, which is a yeast-base cake, much more involved to prepare. Make the day before—garnish with cream the day of the party—keep refrigerated.

The cream can be replaced by ice cream or both can be omitted and the rum cake "flambé with more rum when ready to serve."

1 box yellow cake mix of your choice
½ cup sugar
½ cup water
½ cup dark rum
1 cup whipping cream
3 tbsp. icing sugar
2 tbsp. dark rum

Butter an 8-inch ring mold pan very thoroughly, then sprinkle with sugar and shake pan to remove excess. Mix the cake according to package directions. Pour enough of the batter into the prepared mold to reach to a little more than half way up the mold. Bake in a preheated oven 25 to 30 minutes or until a toothpick inserted in the cake comes out with no batter clinging to it. Let stand on cake rack for 10 minutes before unmolding.

While cake is baking, combine the sugar with the water, stir over medium heat until sugar is dissolved. Take off the heat and stir in the rum. Unmold the cake on to a service plate and pour the hot syrup over the hot cake, it will soak in immediately. If any syrup remains on the plate, spoon it gradually on the cake. Do not refrigerate, even overnight.

To serve, fill center of ring with the cream, whipped and flavored with the sugar and rum. Garnish cream with rose petals or candied violets.

MY FAVORITE BRUNCH

Surprise tomato juice *or*
Sliced oranges in the pink
Cheese Omelette Baveuse
Bouquets of crisp watercress
Paper-thin slices of cold ham
Toasted French bread, unsalted butter
Homemade currant jam
Earl Grey Tea

Surprise Tomato Juice

Peel 1 medium-size cucumber and grate finely, removing the seeds as they accumulate on the grater. Add to 5 or 6 cups of tomato juice with 1 tsp. of sugar, salt and pepper to taste. Refrigerate a few hours or overnight.

When ready to serve, add the juice of ½ a lemon, or 1 tbsp. of Worcestershire sauce or ½ cup of dry gin or vodka. Serve strained or unstrained over ice cubes in cocktail glasses.

Sliced Oranges in the Pink

Peel 6 or 7 oranges and slice as thinly as possible. Place them in a cut glass dish. Thaw out a box of sliced, sweetened strawberries, pour over the oranges but do not mix. Cover and leave overnight at room temperature and stir together just before serving.

Cheese Omelette Baveuse

This is the French type of creamy omelette—an easy and successful way to make a light 6-egg omelette.

6 eggs
6 tbsp. cold water or milk
3 tbsp. butter
½ cup Swiss or mild Cheddar cheese, grated
2 tbsp. Parmesan cheese, grated
1 tbsp. parsley, minced

127

Beat the eggs with the water, then salt and pepper to taste. Melt the butter over high heat in a teflon lined frying pan. Pour in the eggs, but don't stir. Lift the pan off the heat slightly and tilt it so that the egg mixture will run to one side and set in a thin film. Lift up this film with a wooden or nylon spatula and let more of the mixture run under it. Keep tilting, first to one side and then to the other, until most of the mixture is set. Some will still be soft in the middle.

Sprinkle the mixed cheeses on top of the omelette, fold and slide it out of the pan onto a hot serving platter. Sprinkle with the parsley and serve with a bowl of watercress. The grated cheese will melt sufficiently while the omelette is being served. Serves 4-6.

USE OF HERBS

HERBS

Herbs enhance, very often improve, and certainly vary the flavor of our daily foods. But their use should always be subtle — a heavy hand can give the bitterness of an off-flavor.

When using herbs for the first time, experiment cautiously. But, since the quantities given in recipes are only suggestions, you can ignore the directions—simply add a pinch, let it simmer a few minutes, then taste and add another pinch if you wish.

Using all the available herbs would only confuse, and even discourage, the beginner, so try to become thoroughly acquainted with the nine basic ones first—bay leaves, thyme, basil, marjoram, mint, sage, summer savory, parsley and chives.

Bay Leaves are sold dried and should be judged by their color—the greener the better.

A bay leaf or two, combined with a few thin slices of unpeeled lemon to flavor a cut-up chicken while it cooks slowly in butter, or is baked in the oven, helps make a superb dinner.

When in doubt about which herb to use, feel safe adding a bay leaf —the flavor pleases everyone.

Thyme is one of the oldest herbs in use. It has a sweet, penetrating and sharply attractive scent but, because of this, it must be used with discretion. A small pinch will give a nice flavor to all types of meats, vegetables and soups.

Some of its uses: with parsley to flavor a bread stuffing for chicken or fish; in the flour used to roll fish fillets before frying; and for veal dishes of all kinds.

A touch of thyme makes for superb clam chowder, homemade or canned; and a good combination for flavoring cooked greens, a salad or a sauce is ¼ tsp. of thyme to each 1 tsp. of grated lemon peel.

Basil is a pleasantly scented and lively herb with a number of uses. It is popular in Italian cuisine and can always be used with pasta and all types of sauces. It is equally successful with tomato dishes, potatoes, cucumbers, sea food, and especially lamb.

A pinch added to eggs when they're being prepared makes beautiful scrambled eggs. A good salad to serve with steak is sliced tomatoes, simply sprinkled with a dash of sugar, a lot of freshly ground pepper and basil to taste.

Try frying mushrooms with a chopped green onion, then adding salt, pepper and basil to taste.

Marjoram is an herb of the mint family, and the very popular oregano is frequently called wild marjoram. Their similarity of flavor makes them interchangeable. Marjoram is very versatile and will enhance the flavor of meats, soups, stuffings, stews, and many vegetables.

For instance, make little pockets in a roast of pork and stuff them with some marjoram (and a bit of garlic if you're so inclined).

Brown pork chops on one side, turn, sprinkle with pepper and a generous amount of marjoram.

Add 1 tsp. of marjoram to your favorite meat loaf mixture, and also add it to your favorite spaghetti sauce, combined with an equal quantity of basil.

If you use canned spaghetti sauce, add a pinch of basil and marjoram and a bit of lemon peel. Simmer the sauce to heat it.

Mint and cucumber have a great affinity; and fresh, frozen or canned green peas enjoy being flavored with it, too.

In India, they make a fresh mint chutney to eat with curry. Simply combine 2 cups of chopped mint leaves, 2 chopped green onions, 3 tbsp. of fresh lemon juice, ½ tsp. of salt, 1 tbsp. of sugar, ⅛ or ¼ tsp. of cayenne. It will keep for several days if it is stored covered in the refrigerator.

Cantaloup, blueberries and raspberries are very fond of mint. For each 1 qt. of cleaned fruit, mix ½ cup of sugar with finely chopped fresh mint to taste. Chopped fresh mint is also good sprinkled on lemon or lime sherbet.

To make mint tea, simply place the fresh or dried mint in a teaspoon, hold it carefully over a glass, and pour boiling water on top. Let it stand for 5 minutes, sweeten to taste and serve hot or cold. If you have made it too strong, dilute with boiling water.

Sage has an affinity for all game birds, as well as pork and veal but, since it's a powerful, assertive herb, some tact is needed in its use —just a little will give a racy tang to braised meat, croquettes and stews.

There is a great deal of difference in the flavor of fresh and dried sage. Both are good, but the fresh is less powerful—experiment.

Combine 2 cups of fresh breadcrumbs, 1 cup of sausage meat, 1 cup of grated unpeeled apples, a bit of chopped onion and ½ tsp. of sage. Salt to taste, and you have a very nice stuffing for wild or domestic duck. Triple the recipe if it's to be for a goose.

Add ½-1 tsp. of sage to your next meat and tomato macaroni, and sprinkle a bit on your sausages when they are almost cooked.

Sprinkle sage over fried onions; it also goes well with lima beans. Combine equal amounts of sage, thyme and marjoram. Keep in an airtight jar and use some when making hot biscuits or homemade bread or cornbread.

Savory is often a confusing term. Winter savory, a perennial, has a more pungent smell, but most dried savory on sale in our markets is the summer type, an annual which is much milder in flavor.

Savory is distinctly aromatic, but it's not as powerful as sage. If you have to be limited, savory and bay leaf could be the only two seasonings in your kitchen because, combined or alone, they can flavor almost any type of food you cook.

In Germany and Holland, savory is always used with fresh green or wax beans, or with dried beans. With the fresh, sprinkle a pinch on top before boiling.

Add ½ tsp. of savory to 1-2 cups of white sauce for creamed cabbage, and mix fine breadcrumbs, lemon peel and savory to coat fish or veal scallops.

Add a pinch to the horseradish sauce to be served with boiled beef, and use savory to flavor hash and split pea soup.

Parsley is surely the most familiar herb of all those in use. But it's regrettable that so many people use it only as a food garnish—and so few eat it.

Parsley is most frequently chopped to flavor and color sauces, or to sprinkle on potatoes, yet it can also be very good when used in large quantities.

My favorite hamburger mix is ½ lb. of ground beef combined with ½ lb. of ground pork, salt and pepper to taste, 1 egg, and 1 cup, yes, a whole cup, of chopped fresh parsley. Shape and broil.

Try rolling boiled beets in butter and lots of chopped parsley; ¼ cup of it added to ½ cup of butter, with fresh chives to taste, is a perfect butter for hot bread.

To me, the crowning glory of parsley is the way the Scandinavians use it to stuff a chicken. Brush the inside of the bird with 1 tsp. of salt mixed with 2 tsp. of cider vinegar or fresh lemon juice. Then stuff as much fresh parsley as you can use into the cavity. Tie up and roast the chicken as usual. Make a sauce by adding ½ cup of chopped parsley to the pan juices.

Chives are not always available if you don't grow them in your garden. They are the most delicate member of the onion family and, except for desserts, can add a happy touch to any dish you prepare. Many who do not like the tang and flavor of onion will enjoy the mild, pleasant taste of fresh chives.

They are delicious blended into creamed cheese, perfect in an omelette, and are at home sprinkled on any green salad.

A hard-boiled egg white sauce is especially elegant with fresh chives added, and so are deviled eggs when chives are blended into the yolks.

IDEAS, QUICK TRICKS
AND SUGGESTIONS

GOURMET IDEAS FOR PREPARED VEGETABLES

Of all foods, we abuse vegetables the most. We let the frozen ones steam their lives away. We let canned green peas turn into little more than yellow rubbery nuggets with no more flavor than warmed-over dumplings. There's more to it than "cook and drain".

Open a Can, Then 1-2-3

Do not drain the liquid from the cans down the sink—some of the vitamins, minerals and soluble proteins have cooked out into it. Instead, drain this tasty liquid into a saucepan, flavor with a pinch of herb, a bit of sugar and a small piece of butter. Then, without covering it, boil rapidly for 5 minutes until the liquid is reduced to less than half its original quantity. Then, just before you are ready to serve them, add the vegetables and simmer (do not boil) for 3 minutes. All canned vegetables can be heated this way.

Frozen Vegetables Are Good—Sometimes Even Better

Frozen vegetables can be used in any way that fresh vegetables are—and you can cook them in even less water and in less time than specified on the packages. Try cooking them this way.

Here's the Basic Method for Frozen Vegetables

If possible use a heavy enameled cast iron pan. In it melt 1 tbsp. butter, add ½ cup water and a pinch of sugar or honey. (The latter compensates for the loss of some of the natural sugar which converts to starch after the vegetables are picked.) Place the frozen block of vegetables in the middle of the boiling water, butter and sugar. Cover the pan, lower the heat and simmer 10-20 minutes turning the vegetables once. Above all, do not overcook. There will be very little liquid left, and this can be evaporated by a few seconds of rapid boiling with the cover off. Then season or cream to taste.

I like to cook frozen squash and pumpkin in a double boiler with 2 tbsp. butter, a pinch of cinnamon or nutmeg, a large spoonful of sour cream and sometimes, for an added flourish, I pour in a few spoonfuls of brandy or rum. Cover, heat, beat and eat—with delight. And delight it will be, I promise.

Frozen corn on the cob I "steam boil" in ¼ cup milk sweetened with ½ tsp. sugar for 20 minutes. I use a heavy, covered saucepan, and keep the heat low. Salt tends to toughen the kernels.

For all other frozen vegetables I like to use an enameled cast iron frying pan with a good cover—a bit of butter and always a minimum of water. When cooked, the water is practically evaporated and the vegetables are beautifully seasoned with the butter. Sometimes, for a creamed effect, I add a large spoonful of sour cream just before serving. For a classical Greek effect, I substitute olive oil for the butter and add fresh lemon juice just before serving. It's good for flavor and digestion.

Season Vegetables with Imagination

One of our greatest mistakes is to take vegetables for granted. When it comes to serving them, too many cooks expect them somehow to look after themselves. Even the humblest vegetables should be treated with respect and affection. Those that you buy frozen or canned have already been given a good start. All you have to do with them now is remember a few basic rules.

To Sweet-Tasting Vegetables such as Cabbage and Greens—add a little lemon or lime juice. Or a pinch of rosemary. Or a few whole cloves. Or a sprinkling of curry.

To Carrots, Potatoes or Turnips—add minced chives or parsley or coarsely ground black pepper. Or a pinch of thyme.

To Spinach—add a little mace or nutmeg. Or a dash of tarragon vinegar. Or a bit of crushed or fried garlic. Or sour cream and sesame seeds.

To Beets—add 2 whole cloves while cooking. Or serve with sour cream or minced green onions. Good with a dash of malt vinegar or a pinch of fresh dill or dill seeds.

To Green Peas or Wax Beans—add the classic touch of finely chopped mint while cooking, or a pinch of summer savory or crisp bacon when ready to serve. Or add a dash of curry.

Any vegetable can be the highlight of a meal with the addition of a little lemon juice, chutney, vinaigrette* or salad dressing. Whichever one you use, add it just before serving.

Vinaigrette sauce is a spiced vinegar, boiled down, and mixed with some white or red wine and some finely cut green onions, tarragon, parsley, and a few drops of lemon juice. Finely cut capers, without their vinegar, can be added to this.

TAKE A CAN OF SEAFOOD—ET, VOILA!

It's not surprising what good eating can be had from canned seafood. There is such a variety on the grocer's shelves. When you consider how versatile salmon, tuna, bonito, lobster, crab, shrimp, oysters and all the other ready-cooked fish can be, you'll use them more and more. Here are a few of my favorite quick seafood dishes.

Six Different Ways to Serve Canned Seafood

Quick Seafood Casserole
Take any canned seafood—lobster, crab, shrimp, oysters—and arrange in a flat baking dish. Add ¼ cup sherry, a sprinkling of tarragon, 2 tbsp. butter cut in small pieces, ¼ cup table cream or ½ cup sour cream. Cover with my favorite crumb topping and bake 10 minutes at 300°.

My Favorite Crumb Topping: Combine ¼ cup crushed crackers, ¼ tsp. paprika, 2 tbsp. melted butter or olive oil, 1 tbsp. crushed potato chips, 2 tsp. grated Parmesan cheese and a pinch of tarragon or thyme.

Fish Pie
Line a pie plate with ready-mixed pastry. Break up the contents of any 7-oz. can of fish or seafood. Add to it 1 cup milk, ½ cup fine soft breadcrumbs, 2 beaten eggs, ½ tsp. curry or dill seeds, a finely chopped onion, salt, pepper and parsley (if you like it). Place this mixture in the crust-lined plate. (Flute the edges nicely.)

Now you have your choice of four finishing touches—either leave it as it is with no crust on top. Or top it with a crust. Or sprinkle the top with ½ cup grated cheese or with ½ cup sour cream beaten into an egg with a dash of nutmeg. No matter which way you choose, the pie bakes 30-35 minutes at 375°. The texture is creamy; the flavor, delicious.

Fish Pie—The Quebec Way

Line a pie plate with ready-mixed pastry. Fill it with mashed potatoes flavored with savory and chopped green onions. Top with a 7-oz. can of salmon or 2 cans of sardines. Cover with a crust, and bake until golden brown at 375°. This makes a good supper.

Sardines à la Basque

Heat 1 or 2 cans of sardines in their own oil. Then drain and arrange them on toast. Toast and sardines are served with small boiled potatoes that have been covered with white sauce or a warmed-up can of undiluted celery soup, then sprinkled with minced parsley, chives or chopped hard-cooked egg.

Sardine Roll Niçoise

Split and lightly butter long crisp rolls. On one half arrange thin slices of tomato and shreds of green pepper or onion rings. On the other half spread 2 or 3 mashed sardines, well seasoned with lemon juice, chopped parsley or garlic. Press the two halves together and serve with a salad.

Fish Casserole Florentine

Boil half of an 8-oz. package of spaghetti. Drain, mix 1 tbsp. butter and arrange in a casserole. Over it spread 2 cups chopped well-drained and seasoned canned spinach. Cover the spinach with the contents of a can of any coarse-flaked fish. Top all with 2 cups white sauce made from 2 tbsp. butter, 2 tbsp. flour, 1 cup milk and the reserved juice drained from the spinach (adding milk if there is less than a cup of spinach liquid). Season with salt and pepper, and when the sauce is cooked add 1 tsp. lemon juice, 1 tbsp. mayonnaise, and a pinch of dill. Sprinkle the casserole with ½ cup grated cheese and bake 30 minutes at 350°. This dish is good the year round and is sure to be a great favorite of your family and guests.

SIX DESSERTS FOR IMPATIENT GOURMETS

Mix a devil's food or chocolate cake according to directions on the package. Then beat in 2 tsp. instant coffee, 1 tsp. cinnamon, ¼ tsp. cloves and 1 tsp. vanilla. Bake in layers. To serve, put slightly softened ice cream (vanilla or chocolate) between the layers.

Broiled Cake

Bake a white cake in a single layer. Remove it from the oven, and while warm spread it with a mixture made up of 3 tbsp. melted butter, 6 tbsp. brown sugar, 2 tbsp. cream, 2 tbsp. sherry, ½ cup shredded coconut, and ¼ cup chopped walnuts. Then put the cake under the broiler a minute or two until golden brown.

Fresh Strawberry Delight

Crush a pint of strawberries lightly—do not mash. Stir for a few minutes with 1 cup sugar and 1 tsp. lemon juice. Pour the strawberries over a cooled angel food cake. Serve with a dish of whipped cream sweetened and flavored with vanilla. Let your guests help themselves.

Banana Cake Dessert

Mix a yellow cake mix as directed on the box. Just before pouring the batter into the pan add 1 cup mashed ripe banana pulp and the grated rind of 1 orange. Bake as directed. Serve with whipped cream and shredded coconut.

Cherry Jubilee Parfait Pie

Add ⅓ cup brandy to the drained contents of a can of pitted dark sweet cherries. Let stand overnight. Save the cherry juice, and the next day heat and add enough boiling water to make 1 cup. In this dissolve 1 package of raspberry gelatine. Add the brandy drained from the cherries. Then stir in by spoonfuls 1 pint of vanilla ice cream—stirring each time until melted. Chill the mixture until slightly thickened. Then fold in the drained cherries. Turn into a baked and cooled 9-inch pie shell. Chill. But don't freeze it too hard.

Eggnog Parfait Pie

Dissolve a package of lemon gelatine in a cup of hot water with 2 tbsp. sugar. Stir in by spoonfuls a pint of vanilla ice cream—stirring until melted. Add 1 tsp. vanilla and 1 tsp. rum flavoring. Chill until half set, then blend in 2 eggs that have been beaten until foamy. Turn into pie shell. Sprinkle with nutmeg and chill. Ice cream pies are best when smooth and not frozen hard.

THE ICE CREAM BAR

All the sauces can be prepared ahead of time and kept refrigerated in serving containers. Set them out with a bucket of ice cream, plates, spoons, and let everybody go to town.

Melba Sauce: Bring to a boil ½ cup of red or black currant jelly, 1 tbsp. of cold water, ⅛ tsp. of salt, ½ cup of raspberry jam, and 1 tbsp. of lemon juice. Remove from heat and let cool before refrigerating. Yield: 1 cup.

Fluffy Tropical Topping: Combine 6 oz. of undiluted frozen orange juice with 1 cup of cream, whipped. Fold in ½ cup of moist, shredded coconut and 1 tsp. of grated orange rind. Yield: 2 cups.

Butterscotch Cream Sauce: Place in a saucepan ¾ cup of sugar, 1⅓ cups of brown sugar, ¾ cup of corn syrup, ¼ cup of butter, and ½ cup of undiluted evaporated milk. Stir constantly over medium heat until sugar is dissolved and sauce well-blended. Add another ½ cup of evaporated milk and stir 1 minute. Cool, then add ½ tsp. of vanilla. Yield: 2-2¼ cups.

Toffee Sauce: This one should be served hot. Place contents of a 1-lb. bag of caramels in the top of a double boiler over water kept hot, but not boiling. Cover and let melt, then stir in ½ cup of hot water. Yield: 2 cups.

Hot Fudge Sauce: Place in a saucepan 3 squares (1 oz. each) of unsweetened chocolate, 1 cup of sugar, 1 cup of corn syrup, ½ cup of light cream or evaporated milk, and 2 tbsp. butter. Cook over medium heat, stirring constantly, until mixture comes to a full rolling boil. Boil briskly 3 minutes, remove from heat and add 1 tsp. of vanilla. If made ahead of time, refrigerate and reheat by placing in a pan of hot, not boiling, water until sauce has thinned to pouring consistency. Yield: 2 cups.

Coffee Ice Cream: The easiest one of all. Simply have your guests sprinkle instant coffee granules to taste over their vanilla ice cream. It's even more scrumptious topped with a chocolate sauce.

If you don't like the idea of a self-serve table, try one of these:

Six ounces of undiluted frozen juice over a brick of chocolate ice cream.

Drained and mashed canned peaches plus grated orange rind over strawberry or vanilla ice cream.

QUICK AND SIMPLE WAYS WITH
FRESH STRAWBERRIES

Some variations for fresh strawberries:

— Cover with brown sugar or grated maple sugar—top with sour cream.
— Sweeten with strawberry jam diluted with hot apple or orange juice.
— Mix equal quantities of strawberries and cubes of fresh pineapple, sweeten to taste and pour fresh orange juice on top.
— Pour over the berries orange juice mixed with finely chopped fresh mint. Sprinkle the whole with icing sugar. Chill thoroughly and serve heaped in fruit cocktail glasses.
— Whip 1 cup cream, fold it into 1 pint of soft strawberry ice cream. Serve over the sweetened berries.
— For delicious, unusual muffins, replace the 1 cup of milk in your favorite muffin recipe with 1 cup crushed sweetened strawberries. Add 1 extra tbsp. butter or shortening.
— Whip 1 cup cream, sweetened with ½ cup clear honey and 2 tbsp. crushed strawberries. Serve with a bowl of berries.

FRUIT

When our fresh fruit season is at its height, satisfy your sweet tooth with some of these. Or simply top the fruit with a cooked grain such as buckwheat.

— Slice unpeeled oranges, then toss with pitted black olives and sweet onion rings. Serve on crisped lettuce topped with lemon-orange dressing (see below).

— Thinly slice peeled and cored pears, add chopped chives or green onions, seedless grapes, a pinch of fennel seeds and serve on lettuce with French dressing.

— Finely chop 8-10 fresh mint leaves, stir with 1 tbsp. of honey and refrigerate at least an hour. One hour before serving, section 4 grapefruits into a glass dish, top with honey-mint and refrigerate again. Stir before serving.

— Frost grapes to eat with lightly buttered whole-grain bread (dark rye, crushed wheat). Spread clear honey on a cluster of grapes, using a pastry brush, then dip in finely ground dry coconut. Small bunches of different colored grapes are very attractive.

— For a delectable uncooked fruit mousse, beat 3 egg whites with ¼ cup of honey until stiff. Without cleaning beaters, beat 3 yolks with another ¼ cup of honey until fluffy. Fold two mixtures together and add 2-4 cups of diced fruits. Top with grated orange rind, finely chopped nuts, and refrigerate. Serves 4.

— For Cherries à la Parisienne, fill a glass bowl with fresh cherries (they don't have to be pitted), top with a few spoonfuls of honey and let stand 4 hours at room temperature. Stir and serve topped with sour cream or yogurt.

— To make lemon-orange dressing for fruit salads, mix ⅓ cup each of fresh orange juice and safflower or peanut oil, ¼ cup of fresh lemon juice, 1 tbsp. of honey, 1 tsp. each of curry powder and salt. Keep refrigerated and shake well before using. Yield: 1¼ cups.

— For a fruit salad French dressing you don't have to refrigerate, mix ¼ cup of fresh lemon or lime juice, 1 tbsp. of sweet vermouth, ¾ cup of peanut oil, 1 tsp. of salt, 1 tsp. of crushed dried mint and, if you wish, ¼ tsp. of crushed dried tarragon. Shake well before using. Yield: 1½ cups.

(You can substitute cider vinegar for the vermouth, but then you have to refrigerate the dressing, and this one, like most, is very much nicer served at room temperature.)

BREAKFAST FRUIT

The following are just a few suggestions for a sparkling start to a Sunday breakfast. I leave my fruit overnight at room temperature to bring out the full flavor, you may prefer to refrigerate it.

Fresh strawberries, sweetened to taste and marinated in fresh orange juice, look lovely served in crystal cups, as do peeled oranges, in slices or sections, topped with chopped pecans or walnuts and a dash of sherry.

Angostura bitters can be used for more than cocktails. Halve a grapefruit, remove seeds, loosen sections, sprinkle each half with 1 heaping tsp. of maple or brown sugar and about 10 drops of bitters. Cover and let stand overnight, or you can wait and prepare it only 10 minutes before serving.

Apples and oranges are also a nice overnight-stand combination. For 6 people, peel 4 oranges and slice thinly. Peel and core 3 apples and slice thinly. Place fruit in alternate layers in a glass dish, sprinkling each layer with sugar (I use a total of ½ a cup in all, you may want more). Sprinkle with the juice of ½ a lime or lemon, cover and let stand.

If you want something exotic and spectacular, serve hot brandied citrus. For 4 people, carefully peel and section 1 large grapefruit and 2 oranges the night before. Arrange layers alternately in a shallow buttered dish and squeeze the juice of 2 oranges on top. Mix 3 tbsp. of brown sugar with ½ tsp. of mace or nutmeg and sprinkle over. Dot the whole with 2 tbsp. of butter, then pour 2-4 tbsp. of brandy on top. When ready to serve, bake for 25 minutes at 325°. This can also be served cold—omit the butter, cover and leave overnight at room temperature. The sugar will melt and form a syrup.

Then there are always moons of cantaloup, with the juice of ½ a lime squeezed on top of each. Sweeten them with fruit sugar if you like.

And finally a delicious combination is to thaw the contents of 1 package of frozen strawberries, pass them through a sieve or blender, and use as a syrup over fresh raspberries.

QUICK TRICKS FOR SUMMER COOKING

In summer's heat, elaborate cooking is just too much for most of us to tackle. At the same time, I find that when people get together in relaxed moments, everyone becomes interested in good eating. So the dining table or patio should be a happy gathering place. There is a solution to this dilemma: quick tricks with ready-made foods, and things that are easy to whip up in your kitchen. When considering these ideas, remember that each one is flexible enough to be given your own personal touch. Create your own ideas from mine.

Quick Tricks with Fresh Vegetables

Lettuce with a Continental Air: Serve a wedge of lettuce with sardines perched on it, garnished with hard cooked eggs and lemon wedges. No dressing. Try vegetable salt (buy at health food shop) and freshly ground pepper with lemon, which give a dew-fresh feeling. Add hot bread and large bowl of berries.

Salad Luncheon: Make individual bowls of crisp lettuce (try romaine), quartered and seeded tomatoes, cottage cheese and lots of crisp bacon broken up in small pieces. Buy, get from your garden, or beg from a neighbor a handful of fresh herbs (basil, marjoram, dill or tarragon) and sprinkle on salad. Toss with French dressing. Serve with crackers, crisped in oven just before serving. End with old-fashioned gingerbread à la mode (made from cake-mix).

Lots of Tomatoes: This is my favorite with all barbecues. For 6 people—quarter 12 unpeeled tomatoes, put them skin side down in large iron frying pan. Add 2 diced onions. Dot generously with butter, sprinkle with good dose of brown sugar or maple sugar, then cook, uncovered, over a really slow fire for a good 1½ hours. Never stir, just shake pan occasionally. Tomatoes become dark brown and luscious! Yes, you can cook them on the barbecue away from the intense heat, in the same frying pan, of course.

Green Peas à la Parisienne: Melt 1 tbsp. butter, add enough shredded lettuce to cover bottom of saucepan, top with few slivers of onion, a pinch of sugar, and the well-drained canned green peas. No salt, please. Cover and simmer 10 minutes.

Canned Beets the Dutch Way: Drain 1 can diced beets, add them to 2 minced onions lightly browned in butter, with 1 tbsp. vinegar, a pinch of sugar, salt and pepper. Heat and serve.

Quick Tricks with Meat

Cold Roast Beef: Slice thinly, oh, so thinly. Serve with a basket of lace potatoes and pot of good strong mustard. To make lace potatoes: Grate and mix together 1 raw potato (wash, do not bother to peel), 1 onion (bother to peel), and drop mixture by spoonfuls into sizzling butter or bacon fat, ½ minute each side; then they are cooked and so pretty.

Your Own Pâté Maison: Fun to serve with Melba toast, when having drinks in the garden. Sauté 5 minutes in butter some chicken livers and minced onion to taste. Then put them through food grinder with 2 hard-boiled eggs. Season with salt, pepper and tarragon or curry, and why not a tablespoon of brandy or Scotch?

The Hamburger We Have Forgotten: Shape freshly ground round steak (ground only once) into 4-inch rounds, about ¼ inch thick. Wrap each one in freezing paper and freeze. Also keep in freezer split onion or poppy seed buns, the large kind. For a quick lunch in the garden, place frozen buns in 400° oven. Unwrap minced steak, season with salt, pepper, paprika, monosodium glutamate. Cook quickly in hot butter, still frozen, 5, 8 or 10 minutes for rare, medium or well-done. Or you can barbecue them. Place in hot buns. Choose your garnish, and enjoy with hot or cold tea.

Leftover Chicken: Make a "Ritz-looking" salad with leftover greens. To 2 cups diced chicken, add 1 cup diced celery, 1 unpeeled diced apple, a handful of seedless grapes. Blend with ½ to 1 cup mayonnaise. Mix with 3 tablespoons to 1 cup mayonnaise. Mix with 3 tablespoons cream, and curry powder to taste. Serve a light, very light, dessert after this.

No Meat, and No Hurry: Make a potato pie. Line pie plate with your favorite packaged pie crust. Make mashed potatoes with those wonderful instant flaked potatoes. Instead of butter, add ½ cup sour cream to potatoes when ready. Place in bottom of crust, top with 1 cup cottage cheese or 1 can salmon. Top with ½ cup sour cream, 1 egg and minced onion to taste, blended together. Then top with pie crust. Bake in 400° oven until golden brown. Good hot or cold. Serve with assorted pickles.

Too Many for Your One Barbecued Chicken?: Well, make a casserole. Heat 1 can undiluted consommé. Place in it your cut-up (in many pieces) barbecued chicken, 1 box frozen peas (in frozen state). Cover and simmer until hot. Line casserole with a 2 to 3-inch layer of that already-cooked rice you have in your refrigerator. Pour chicken, green peas and consommé on top. Then, add 1 can mushroom soup mixed with ½ cup cream. Bake 25 minutes in 350° oven. And you are ready to serve 6 instead of 2.

Quick Tricks with Sauces and Soups

English Cucumber Sauce: Are you serving one of those fabulous fresh boiled salmons, cold or hot? Try my cucumber sauce, that I found in London, England, years ago. Have all ingredients very cold before you start. Peel and grate 1 cucumber. Whip ½ cup cream, add very slowly 2 tablespoons tarragon vinegar, gradually beating all the time. Season. Just before serving, mix in grated cucumber.

Quick Vichyssoise: In your blender put 1 can frozen potato soup, and 1 can milk or cream. Place in covered saucepan, 2 leeks or onions, sliced, and melt in 2 tablespoons butter for 10 minutes. Then, add to soup in blender. Cover and blend 1 minute. Taste for seasoning. Refrigerate until ready to serve.

Superb Gravy and Vegetables: All in one, for your roast lamb or beef. Remove roast from drippings, but do not remove any of the fat. Place pan over direct heat. Add I can undiluted consommé, 1 box frozen green peas (not thawed out), and sometimes 1 tablespoon tomato paste; at another time, 1 tablespoon rye or Scotch. Stir over medium heat until peas are tender, about 8 to 10 minutes.

Quick Tricks with Sour Cream

I love sour cream (the commercial type).

— Call it Devonshire Cream, and pour it over berries, sprinkled with maple sugar.

— Add a large, large, spoonful to your veal or chicken gravy, blend but do not boil.

— Top your cold soup with it, sprinkle with chives.

— Melt a package of chocolate chips, pour while hot over ½ cup sour cream. Stir. It makes a divine ice cream sauce or sponge cake topping. Or you can serve it with pears.

— Perfect dressing for summer vegetable salad.

— A dream on cucumbers. To 1 cup sour cream, add 1 teaspoon salt, 2 tablespoons tarragon vinegar (or use what you have), 1 teaspoon dry mustard, 1 teaspoon sugar, ½ teaspoon paprika.

Quick Tricks for Dessert

Classic of Haute Cuisine with Plain Canned Food: Drain canned pitted Bing cherries, peaches and pineapple chunks. Mix the juices. Add juice of 1 lemon to 1 cup of mixed fruits. For the "haute cuisine" touch, add brandy to taste, but be lavish with it. Serve cool, cool!

French Chef Special: A bought ready-made chiffon cake. Roll cake in 1 cup maple syrup beaten with ¼ cup rum. (Yes, a bit sticky.) Then roll cake in finely shredded coconut, or finely chopped nuts. Top with rum-flavored whipped cream.

Shortcake in 5 Minutes: Place a bought, ready-made, double-layer sponge cake in a 350° oven for 5 minutes, just to heat. Squeeze juice of 2 oranges (no law against adding a little rum to it). Slowly pour orange juice over hot cake. Pour 1 box thawed-out frozen berries on top. No cream is needed. Delicious just exactly as it is.

TEA DAINTIES

Quick ideas for unexpected guests at tea time.

— Hovis bread or any good brown bread well buttered and sprinkled with one's favorite fresh herbs.

— Small slices of French bread buttered covered with a thin slice of Swiss or Cheddar cheese. Sprinkle with basil or tarragon. Brown under broiler. Serve hot or cold.

— White bread buttered with cream cheese or cottage cheese, top with honey, serve on a bed of mint. Guests eat mint with bread or sprinkle mint on honey.

— Bread or hot biscuits buttered with foie gras sprinkled with tarragon.

AN EASY WEEKEND
WITH GUESTS

People change when they become guests. At home they can live on a steady diet of sameness, but when they visit, they psychologically change and tend to eat more, drink more and sleep more. With this in mind, here are my rules:

— Meals should be planned ahead and so designed that half your work is done before the weekend.

— The dangerous time in a weekend is the hour before dinner. I am sure that, like me, you have sat in someone's living room, watching the clock crawl and conversation fade. A cool beer, a dry martini, a fresh sherry, or a gay hostess (not strained by kitchen worry) can always make this hour happy.

— Guests sleep more, and why can't you? You can have your morning to yourself if you tell your female guests you will serve them a delicious brunch on Saturday or Sunday. Rarely will you get an objection from them for being allowed to sleep in. And you will find fixing a tray is quicker than setting the table for many. As for the male guest, his natural independence and habit will probably prevail, and so have a tray ready for him in the kitchen and let him rise as early as he wants for his fishing or golfing.

— Guest rooms must have ashtrays, matches, cigarettes (if you like), a few interesting magazines or books (a must), a bouquet of flowers, a good bed, and emergency blankets for cool nights.

— Don't offer three big meals a day. For most weekends I have made the evening meal the big one. I leave fruit, milk, cake or cookies within easy reach for the midnight refrigerator raiders— with cups and glasses, spoons, knives and attractive paper napkins handy on a tray.

— To simplify my marketing, I prepare my weekend menu and make a complete list of all I shall need, way ahead of time. I pin the menu in the kitchen for easy reference.

— Plan some activities that you can enjoy together, and others that you can do separately.

Friday Welcome Snacks

Your guests arrive Friday after supper. When they are settled, a drink and a light snack will start off their visit with you on the right note. Choose the drinks according to your fancy, or theirs. As for the snacks, here are two easy-to-make ideas:

Viva Italia

Serve a ready made pizza, cut in small wedges—each wedge topped with a smoked sardine, hidden under a slice of cheese, and the whole sprinkled with basil or marjoram. Heat in 350° oven when guests are ready for it. Use attractive paper napkins, and a round, shallow basket to hold the aluminum plate the ready pizza comes in. It saves washing plates and a platter. When finished, throw out the aluminum plate and napkins; hang up the basket. Perfect served with cold beer.

Summer Gala

Or, make your entrance with fresh peaches in champagne, or sparkling wine, or port wine, or vin rosé. To lazily munch with this, offer lovely light biscuits such as: doigts de dame, champagne fingers, or little langues de chats. Look for them in the fancy biscuit shelves of gourmet shops. Oh! yes, the peaches. Peel and slice them thinly, sugar ever so lightly, place in a covered glass jar and refrigerate until ready to make your entrance. Then place a fair portion of the peaches in a cool champagne glass or old-fashioned glass, and fill the glass with the chosen wine. If your mood is such, top with a rose petal, or a violet.

Saturday Lunch

If you plan to take your guests out and include lunch in town, I have one suggestion: choose an interesting restaurant beforehand, make reservations, and even order lunch for all. This will give your guests a feeling of really being entertained with elegance.

If you plan to lunch at home, make it a light lunch, buffet style. And why not serve it in the kitchen, as I often do? This should be the one effortless meal of the weekend. So follow a menu in which there will be no cooking—or just the minimum. You'll have everything in the refrigerator, ready to serve.

My kitchen buffet lunches are always fun. I try to serve them with a flourish—usually writing what is served on a small blackboard hanging over the table.

Menu for an Easy Cold Lunch

Ring-Around-the-Rosy
Snow in the Summer
Tipsy Seventh Cloud Cake

Ring-Around-the-Rosy

On Friday morning, boil separately some beets, unpeeled potatoes, and young carrots. When cooked, peel and slice them. Place in separate bowls. Blend each one with your favorite French dressing. Cover and refrigerate. Mince an equal quantity of parsley and celery leaves; mix and place in a covered glass container.

After breakfast on Saturday, take all of it out of the refrigerator. Choose a colorful meat platter, fill the middle with attractive dollops of carrots, beets and potatoes. Surround with boiled eggs, rolled first in mayonnaise, then in parsley and celery leaf mixture, until they look like "green eggs". Place around the vegetable posy. Cover whole dish, and take out of refrigerator when it's lunchtime.

Snow in the Summer

Late Friday afternoon, grind very fine 4 tbsp. blanched almonds or walnuts. Add 2 tbsp. rosewater, grated peel of 1 orange, ½ cup white wine, nutmeg to taste, and a pinch of rosemary, if you have it. Pour ½ pint whipping cream over the whole. Blend very well. Cover and refrigerate until you are ready to serve. Strain and add fruit sugar to taste, about 2 to 3 tbsp. is about right, and whip until frothy. Pour into light glass dish — it will look like snow. Keep refrigerated until serving time.

Tipsy Seventh Cloud Cake

Buy a white angel-food cake or make one on Thursday or Friday from your favorite cake mix (they keep very well). When you whip your Snow in the Summer, take the same white wine and saturate the cake with at least 1 cup. Sprinkle with instant cocoa. To serve, break off a piece with two forks and top with Snow in the Summer.

Saturday Dinner

Come sundown, cast a magic spell for your guests with a romantic candlelight supper. Of course, all the children are in bed, even if it means eating at 9:30 p.m. — who cares in the summer? Oh, yes, the children have to be fed first: why not send them into the garden at 6 p.m., or the terrace or the balcony — with a picnic box? Let them enjoy themselves, maybe fight together a bit. Come 7 or 8 p.m., they should be ready for bed. Then you see to the finishing touches of your showcase of delight for the grown-up dinner — try to fix it so that you can enjoy a tall cool drink with the others. Here is one of those dinners you may use, as I have, "happily ever after."

Iced Soup Rosée Héloïse
Coq au Vin
Rice Paprika
Potted French Garden Green Peas
Authentic English Trifle

Iced Soup Rosée Héloïse

Peel 2 lbs. fresh tomatoes by first pouring boiling water over them. Cut them in half and press through a metal sieve to extract all juice and pulp possible. Add juice of 1 orange and half a lemon, 1 wine glass white wine, and 1 tsp. sugar, plus salt and pepper. Blend well together. Refrigerate 6 to 8 hrs. or more, if you wish. Pour from a glass jug into champagne glasses with an ice cube in each glass. If you have the time and the inclination, make frozen flower ice cubes by placing a small fresh flower in each square of the ice tray, fill with boiled, cooled water — and freeze. Nasturtiums, borage or violets are very pretty for this. Place flower cubes in glasses set on a tray and pour the soup as you come to each guest.

Coq au Vin

Remove fat from a 4 to 4½ lb. boiling fowl. Melt fat in large saucepan. Cut fowl in individual pieces, brown all over in fat. Remove pieces to a plate. In their place put 8 small peeled onions and 8 small whole carrots. Sprinkle with ½ tsp. sugar and brown very lightly. Add 1 clove crushed garlic and stir in 3 tbsp. flour. Blend well. Gradually add 2 cups dry red wine, 1 small bay leaf, ¼ tsp. thyme and savory. Bring to boil, stirring all the time. Then, add 1 small can button mushrooms with its liquid. Place chicken pieces into this sauce. Cover and cook 2 to 3 hours, over low heat. Just simmer, do not boil. When chicken is tender, it is ready. Remember that dishes cooked with wine are better if allowed to get cold, then reheated.

Rice Paprika

Boil 1 lb. rice according to directions on package. Mix together 4 tbsp. butter and 1 tbsp. paprika. Blend in cooked rice with a fork, until each grain is coated with the red butter. Serve garnished with a ring of parsley around the dish.

Potted Fresh Garden Green Peas

Shell 2 to 3 lbs. fresh green peas. Place in glass canning jar. Add ½ tsp. sugar, 1 tbsp. butter, a few sprigs of fresh mint. Cover. To cook, place jar in cold water in high saucepan like the bottom of a double boiler. Bring water to a boil, cover saucepan and simmer 1 hour. Do not open jar before ready to serve. Just leave in hot water, if you are not ready. Do *not* salt, pepper or drain the peas.

Authentic English Trifle

First, make a soft rich custard. Beat 4 egg yolks until light and pale yellow. Heat 2 cups light cream with ¼ cup sugar and 1 tbsp. orange flower water or vanilla. Add beaten egg yolks, while beating very hard. Then cook without boiling, stirring continuously until custard coats the spoon. Remove to a bowl. Cover and refrigerate until well chilled.

Cut a two layer sponge cake (that you bake or buy) into finger-length pieces. Spread each one on one side with raspberry jam and quickly dip in ½ cup sherry. Place half these sponge fingers in the bottom of a deep cut-glass bowl. Cover with half the custard. Whip 2 cups cream, sweeten with ½ cup icing sugar and vanilla to taste. Cover custard with half the whipped cream. Make a second layer on top of all this. Top with a dozen or so toasted almonds, standing them upright in the cream, and a few slivers of angelica — or use small roses instead of almonds and angelica. Refrigerate at least 12 hours.

This beautiful dessert never fails to create a sensation, yet it is so easy to prepare.

On Sunday, Sleep In

When you go to bed Saturday night, you won't be in a hurry to get back to your apron and become the hostess again. So do like the others (your guests and your husband). Sleep in Sunday to your heart's content. If you have a little girl, who is sweet and nice, and old enough to take care of the others' breakfast, then of course you can. But there's another way.

Let the early risers look after themselves. Have ready instant coffee, fruit, buns or doughnuts. Show them the night before where things are. Then sleep in peace on Sunday morning.

And now, what about the other Sunday meals? Because most weekend guests leave early in the afternoon, a good brunch served late should be enough. Here again you should have only one dish to cook at the last minute. The rest should be things bought ready-cooked or prepared by you ahead of time. My most popular brunch has everything in it, except the eggs, cooked or prepared right at the table. The menu is:

Cantaloup
Whipped Cream Chicken Livers
or **Eggs Bercy**
Bread or buns with jam, jelly or marmalade
Coffee

Don't say "perish the thought" about Whipped Cream Chicken Livers. They are delicious, and you will find you can never make enough. The alternative, Eggs Bercy, is down-to-earth baked eggs with sausages and tomato sauce.

Whipped Cream Chicken Livers

So rich, but so good!

Clean 1 lb. (about 15) chicken livers, roll in flour. Melt 4 tbsp. butter in electric frying pan. Raise the heat and brown livers in this butter quickly. Add salt, pepper, tarragon, or basil to taste. Have a plate full of toast triangles, unbuttered. In a bowl, pour 1 cup whipped sour or fresh cream, and mix with 1 tbsp. onion, ½ tsp. salt. Place about ⅓ cup of the cream on each warmed plate, and fill centre with cooked livers. Garnish with toast points. And serve with pride.

Be Creative: Replace chicken liver with diced calves liver or diced blanched sweetbreads. Add a little sherry or a sprinkling of nutmeg instead of tarragon or basil.

Replace whipped cream with a cheese or mushroom sauce, or freshly cooked asparagus, and remember the whole can be cooked right at the brunch table in the modern chafing dish, the electric frying pan.

Eggs Bercy

Melt some butter. For each portion, put 1 tsp. of melted butter in bottom of an individual dish or custard cup. Break in an egg carefully and spoon a little melted butter on top. Prepare as far ahead as you wish, but remember the eggs take 15 minutes to cook in a 350° oven. So, time yourself accordingly. While they are cooking, pan fry cocktail sausages or large ones cut up in three. When almost done, sprinkle with a pinch of marjoram, the aroma will delight everyone. Have a bowl of hot tomato sauce, or chili sauce warmed up with a bit of curry powder and sherry added. To serve, place a few sausages over the cooked egg, sprinkle with minced chives or parsley and let each one help himself to the sauce.

Be creative: Put a thin slice of cheese in bottom of dish, break egg on top, bake same way.

Or, quickly pass in hot butter, some fresh, thinly sliced mushrooms, put in bottom of dish, finish as above.

Or, sprinkle cooked egg with minced fresh basil, or diced crisp bacon.

Or, simmer your sausages for 5 minutes in a bit of beer, then brown.

Or, simmer sausages 5 minutes in apple juice. Drain, wrap each one with a slice of bacon. Fry.

Or, replace the tomato sauce with broiled half tomatoes, sprinkled with basil.

HOW TO FIX YOUR MISTAKES IN THE KITCHEN

You weren't paying attention and now you've got a burned stew or overcooked cabbage. Or you want to thicken a sauce and there's not a speck of flour or cornstarch in the house.

The solution can be found here, along with other ways to mend your mistakes. But also included are ways to prevent mistakes, and this is truly the important part of cooking. The well-organized Chinese cook who has everything washed, cut, trimmed, measured, and on hand before he begins is the example we should all try to follow.

Prevention means taking the time to get ready before you start. Besides, a sound knowledge of how to get from A to B in the kitchen makes the actual cooking all the easier.

Eggs

Eggs aren't as uncomplicated as they seem — a lot can go wrong with them. Two ways in particular to look after them are to store them the same way they're packaged (with the small point down, which keeps the yolk in the middle) and to never add salt while they're cooking. Add it only when they're served, salt will toughen them otherwise.

Hard-boiled eggs: If yours come out with the yolk along one side instead of neatly in the middle, you're probably cooking them in too small a pan. Put them into lots of cold (not boiling) water in a pan with plenty of space and they should come out fine.

Eggs sticking to carton: Simply set the carton in a pan of cold water for a few minutes. Keep eggs refrigerated in a bowl and use as soon as possible in case the moisture has affected them.

Yolk in egg whites: The least bit will prevent beaten whites from stiffening properly. You can use a piece of broken shell to pick up the yolk, but the chef's way is best — moisten a corner of a cloth in cold water and just touch the yolk with it. The yolk will cling as if to a magnet.

Volume in egg whites: They'll increase more in size if they're at room temperature before they're beaten. You can use an ordinary wire whisk, a hand rotary beater or an electric mixer, but for high volume and perfect texture, nothing can replace hand beating with the big double balloon wire whisk made especially for whipping cream or egg whites.

Egg yolk as thickener: Like flour and cornstarch, egg yolks can be used as a thickening agent for such things as sauces, custards and cream soups. Two yolks equal 1 tbsp. of flour, and they must be cooked over very gentle heat. Stir 1 tbsp. of cold liquid or hot sauce into the yolks before you add them and stir constantly until the texture is velvety and creamy. Never let the sauce boil.

Overcooked scrambled eggs: You can't rescue them, but you can use them. Keep cooking until they're dried up, let cool, then chop to use over lettuce or canned salmon, or to mix with diced celery and mayonnaise for an egg salad.

Sugar

To brown pot roast meat beautifully, use this chef's trick: Add 1 tbsp. of sugar to a few tablespoons of heated fat and cook over medium heat until sugar browns lightly. Add meat and brown on all sides; the sugar will give it a delectable flavor as well as color.

Hard lumpy sugar: Steam it in the top of a double boiler, then crush it with a spoon, spread it on a tray and let cool. Or put the sugar in a brown paper bag, close tightly and set in a 350° oven. When the bag is warm, the sugar should be soft enough to de-lump — just pass a rolling pin over the bag, then spread the sugar to cool.

Cooking vegetables: Add a pinch of sugar to the cooking water to bring out their finest flavor. Add salt only when serving.

Equivalents: One pound of icing sugar equals 3½ cups, sifted, 1 lb. of brown sugar equals 2¼ cups, firmly packed; and 1 lb. of granulated sugar equals 2 cups.

Salt

It pays to be cautious when using salt; it's difficult to subtract from a dish, but it can always be added. And it should be added to eggs or vegetables only after they've been cooked. Remember too that any simmering liquid becomes saltier as it cooks. Beef and chicken stocks should be salted lightly because the stock must be reduced for the best flavor and this concentrates the salt flavor as well.

Too salty sauce or soup: Can sometimes be brought back to normal by simmering an unpeeled potato, washed and quartered, in the liquid for 15 minutes. Discard the potato, add a pinch of sugar, stir and taste.

Too salty potatoes: Drain off the cooking water and pour fresh boiling water over them. Stir a few seconds and drain again. This will usually remove enough of the salt to make them palatable.

Parsley

Even if it's a bit limp when you buy it you can revive it. Wash in cold water, shake well and refrigerate in a covered glass jar. It will keep crisp and green for 4-5 days.

Stew

You've burned it. Immediately put 5-6 ice cubes in another pot, pour contents of burned pot (without scraping bottom) over them and let simmer on low heat until sauce is hot. The smell and taste of burning will be gone (and all you'll have left to do is clean the original pot).

Potatoes

In late winter, before the new potatoes are available, you'll sometimes find you've bought potatoes that develop black spots when they're cooked. This happens because the frost has gotten to them. The next time you use potatoes from the same bag, start cooking them in cold water to which you've added 1 tsp. of vinegar or 2 slices of unpeeled lemon, and boil them uncovered.

Cabbage

Because cabbage needs very little cooking, it's easy to overdo the job and difficult to remedy. You can add diluted canned consommé and grated cheese to make a soup; or cover the cabbage with a thick white sauce and grated cheese (cheese will always take away most of its strong taste), or add the cabbage to mashed potatoes.

Lettuce

Don't cut out the core or remove the leaves with knife — that's what causes rust. Twist the core to remove and pluck off the leaves. To store, place a few towels in the bottom of a plastic bag in which you've punched 4 or 5 holes. Clean lettuce before adding to bag — the paper will absorb the excess moisture.

Grapefruit

If you have a hard time removing the white skin when peeling these, first boil the grapefruit for 5 minutes in enough water to cover. Let cool, then peel — all the white skin should come away too. Or just pour boiling water over grapefruit, let stand 5 minutes, then peel. And try grapefruit juice in place of vinegar in an oil and vinegar dressing. It's a pleasant change.

Tea

If, come summer, your iced tea gets cloudy, add a spoonful of boiling water to each glass. And for making large quantities of tea, see the section on nylon net (below).

Liver

To tenderize it and to prevent dryness, soak liver 1-4 hours in enough milk to cover. Drain, roll in flour, and fry over medium heat in butter or oil. And chicken livers won't splatter during cooking if you perforate them all over with a fork before you start.

Olives and Pickles

When you've used the first few olives or pickles, float a teaspoon of salad oil on top of the liquid in the jar, cover and refrigerate — they'll keep for a year. The oil forms an airtight cover so no scum can form, and it won't mix with the pickle juices.

Odds and Ends

Glasses: When two are stuck together, put cold water in the top glass and place the bottom in hot water. They'll come apart easily after a few seconds.

Nylon Net: Learn how useful this can be in the kitchen. When a recipe calls for straining through a fine strainer or cheese-cloth, nylon net not only works beautifully, it's easy to rinse, dry and re-use. Net also is handy for making giant size tea bags if you're making large quantities for a party. Fold in several thicknesses, add quantity of tea required and tie with a string. The bag can be re-used many times.

Refrigerators and deep freezers: To keep them smelling sweet, put a lump of charcoal in them. I put mine in a plastic ice cream container through which I've punched air holes with an ice pick. If food has already spoiled, place a pan of uncompressed charcoal in the main part of the refrigerator or freezer. Put fresh charcoal in the next day and leave the first out in the sun to dry for use the third day. The charcoal will gradually absorb the odors.

INDEX